SINNER'S CREED

LEAD SINGER OF CREED

SCOTT STAPP

WITH DAVID RITZ

SINNER'S
A MEMOIR
CREED

Tyndale House Publishers, Inc.
Carol Stream, Illinois

Library of Congress Cataloging-in-Publication Data

Stapp, Scott, date.
  Sinner's creed / Scott Stapp with David Ritz.
    ISBN 978-1-4143-6456-8 (hc)
  1. Stapp, Scott, 1973- 2. Rock musicians—United States—Biography. 3. Creed (Musical group) 4. Christian biography. I. Ritz, David. II. Title.
    ML420.S81168A3 2012
    782.42166092—dc23
    [B]   2012024836

ISBN 978-1-4143-7826-8 (International Trade Paper Edition)

Printed in the United States of America

18	17	16	15	14	13	12
7	6	5	4	3	2	1

I dedicate this book to Jaclyn, Jagger,
Milan, Daniel, Hayat "Yuma," and Jon Paul.
Each of you is a gift from God. I love you with all my heart.

Contents

For a long time I believed in irreconcilable divisions—good and evil, heaven and hell, absolute right and absolute wrong. There was no gray in the world where my morality was molded.

Gaining God's love required work. Pleasing Him meant demonstrating near-perfect behavior. God's demands were not subject to negotiation or alteration. God's commandments, as revealed in His Word to Moses on Mount Sinai, were written in stone by the finger of the Almighty Himself.

The law was the law.

But somewhere deep down, I knew there was also love, the most wondrous of all human and divine qualities. If we are the creations of a loving God, shouldn't that love be the law that guides us? And if we are to love—love God, love others, love ourselves—doesn't that require compassion, patience, and understanding, qualities that defy an ethical order based strictly on ironclad law?

For a long time I didn't allow such questions to enter my consciousness. I challenged their legitimacy. I dismissed them as diversionary tactics concocted by a clever enemy. I couldn't tolerate the uncertainty they created. I couldn't live without uncompromising clarity.

And yet the story of my life is profoundly unclear. It is a rock-and-roll story and, at the same time, a story of my walk with Christ. The two are melded together in ways both unpredictable and unsure.

What remains clear, though, is my passion for the God of love. That passion saw me through. In every stage of my journey, that passion never died. I did compromise my principles through acts that were destructive to myself and harmful to others, but I never lost my faith.

This, then, is my simple testimony:

That God is real.

That I am His child.

That I'm grateful for His boundless mercy and loving grace.

That by confessing my frailties and my sin, I can embrace new freedom and deeper forgiveness.

And that this book, written in the blood of a Christian who lost his way in the maze of life on earth, is dedicated to Him.

Scott Stapp
FALL 2012

SOUTH BEACH is the hippest section of Miami Beach, and the Delano, where a suite can cost $4,000 a night, is one of its slickest hotels. I didn't know it at the time, but that is where I went to die.

This was after the first three Creed albums—*My Own Prison*, *Human Clay*, and *Weathered*—had sold more than thirty million copies worldwide. My solo album, *The Great Divide*, had been released the year before and had gone platinum. For more than a decade I'd been the front man for one of the most popular rock-and-roll bands in the world. My precious son, Jagger, was eight, and in answer to my prayers, I'd married Jaclyn Nesheiwat, the woman of my dreams, in February of that year. I had gone from the poverty of my youth to considerable wealth—and I was only thirty-three. How could things be any better?

How could things be any worse? I'd been assailed by a battery of pernicious drugs—prednisone for my ailing throat, OxyContin for the injuries sustained in a car accident—whose side effects fueled my undiagnosed chronic depression. I was a mess.

Beyond that, the brotherhood of our band had collapsed. Lifelong friendships were shattered; feelings were smashed; jealousy and greed had replaced the innocent dreams of college boys who just wanted to rock and roll. Our modest hope had been to make a living making music—we'd never counted on making a fortune. Yet our fortune seemed to have done us in. We were unprepared for the pressures and pitfalls of overnight success. It was all too soon, too heady, too much.

Drinking—especially binge drinking—had become my way of coping with confusion. And because I was prone to blackouts, bingeing provided the ultimate escape. I realized it was also the ultimate irresponsibility, but that realization only fed my guilt. My guilt fueled my self-contempt, and my self-contempt whispered in my ear, *Why not? You're a miserable moral failure anyway. Why not ruin everything you've worked for? That's all you deserve—humiliation and failure.*

That thinking had me running from the prospect of a happy home life and a rapidly expanding career in music. It also allowed me to ignore the kinds of spiritual questions that had plagued me for years.

"Aren't you a Christian band?" people kept asking me.

"No," I said. "We're a rock-and-roll band. We don't proselytize. We don't evangelize. We just play rock and roll."

"But your lyrics are filled with Christian imagery and Christian thoughts."

"Yes, because I write the lyrics and I'm a Christian."

"Then you *are* a Christian band."

"I'm just one of the four guys."

"If you're writing and singing Christian lyrics, shouldn't you be living a Christian life?"

The easy answer should have been yes. I knew that my drunken behavior was incompatible with my beliefs. At the same time, I had never announced myself as some kind of Christian role model. My rock-and-roll hero was Jim Morrison. I also loved U2 and Bono. *Bono is a Christian,* I thought. *Why isn't his band regarded as a Christian band?* I didn't understand why Creed got burdened with that label.

Or was the burden really a blessing in disguise? These were

questions I could not answer. They served only to confuse me and to drive me back to the bottle.

* * *

In Miami Beach that November, I had been awake for days. Beyond the booze, there was an array of drugs, all easily accessible on South Beach's nightlife scene. But by then, alone in my hotel room, party joy had been replaced by paranoia. I was hearing noises that weren't there. I was sure the sirens of cop cars were blaring just outside.

I became convinced the police were right on my heels. *That must be them on their way up the elevator! Now they're running down the hallway, approaching my door, getting ready to break it down. They're about to arrest me!* I had to escape.

I rushed to the balcony of my room, sixteen stories above the street. My only getaway was to leap from my balcony to the one below. I stood at the edge and looked down. There were sixteen stories between me and the street. It was crazy to jump, but I was sure I heard banging on the door. I couldn't let the cops see me in this condition. I'd be arrested, and the press would eat me alive. What would my family say? My fans? My God? I had to do something. And I did.

I climbed over the railing and hung from the ledge, trying to maneuver down to the next balcony. Then all at once I lost my grip. I fell twenty feet and landed on my forehead. I found out later I'd fractured my skull and broken my hip, arm, and nose. The only reason I hadn't fallen to my death was the presence of a thin concrete ridge twenty feet below, installed to protect the balcony from bird waste. I was now facedown in bird waste, still conscious and in excruciating pain. Looking back, I now know I was face-to-face with what I had become.

I managed to lift my head and saw that the nearest guest room appeared to be unoccupied. I yelled for help, but no one responded. At that moment, I thought no one would find me. I thought I would surely die.

I started screaming out loud to God as though He were on the ledge right in front of me. My words were delusional, my thoughts scattered. "How could You allow all this to happen to me?" I yelled. "You know I love You and my heart's in the right place. Why didn't You protect me? Do You know what humiliation this is going to bring to me? I'm going to be another one of those Christians who embarrass You. Listen, just take my life. I don't care. But please spare my wife and son from shame. They've been through enough. I'll never understand why You would bless me so much only to take it all away."

I felt like I was in the middle of an epic battle between God and Lucifer, good and evil, life and death. At that moment I couldn't deny that the devil had complete control over me, but I also knew I had a heart that loved God. At many times throughout my life, I felt I was living under His divine control and following His purposes for me. So how could the devil have won? This wasn't the way my story was supposed to end.

I struggled to keep my eyes open. Closing them would have meant surrender. The longer my eyes were open, I reasoned, the greater my chance of being discovered. I had to maintain consciousness. I had to be found.

Two hours later, with my eyes still open and the pain reaching unbearable limits, I saw a light turn on in the room below. I could make out shadows of people. One was walking toward the balcony. I used every last ounce of energy at my command to call out, but with the balcony door closed, my cry wasn't loud enough to get the person's attention. He kept walking from one side of the room to the other, never looking up in my direction.

"Help me!" I screamed. "Help me!"

Finally the balcony door opened. As it did, I leaned my head over the edge, and a puddle of blood splattered at the feet of the gentleman standing there. He looked up toward the ledge. I saw his face and thought, *Wait a minute, I know this guy.*

He was wearing a baseball cap with the University of Alabama logo. Don't ask me why, but the only words I was able to whisper were "Roll Tide," referring to the University of Alabama Crimson Tide football team.

He saw my face. "Scott Stapp?" he said. "Man, you messed up."

"I know, brother. Help."

I then looked to heaven and thanked God for loving me.

What were the chances that T.I.—the great rapper, whom I knew from doing songs on a companion album to Mel Gibson's *The Passion of the Christ*—would walk in off the street, check in to the last available room, and arrive just in time to save my life?

"Look, man," he said. "I don't know how you got here, but no cops. You don't want nothing in the news. I'll call an ambulance and get you out of here. I don't know your name—if you know what I mean."

When the medics arrived, they had to use ropes and pulleys to get me off the ledge. Then they put me on a gurney, which turned out to be a major operation. One of the paramedics recognized me immediately and covered me with a sheet so I wouldn't be identified. They carried me through the lobby filled with South Beach revelers in full party mode.

When we got into the ambulance, one of the paramedics said, "I'm a Creed fan. I love you guys. But I gotta ask you something— you weren't trying to kill yourself, were you?"

"No."

"You certain?"

"Absolutely not a suicide. I had too much to drink, and I fell."

"A police officer is going to be here soon," the paramedic said. "That's routine procedure. We're going to clean you up before he gets here. We'll confirm that this was not a suicide attempt, and we'll report it as an accident."

He looked at me and winked. "You have no ID, right?"

"Right."

"Forget your name. You don't want this in the papers. But believe me, man, I've never seen anyone survive a fall like that."

When I got to the trauma center in Miami, the doctors reached the same conclusion. "We have no medical explanation for why you're alive. A human skull is not strong enough to survive that kind of direct impact. Your head should have cracked open like a watermelon. It may take you a full year to recover. You're going to have to relearn how to walk, and it won't be easy. The truth is, you've suffered a severe skull fracture so deep that air entered your brain."

"So I'm officially an airhead?" I managed to joke.

"You're officially the luckiest man I've ever seen."

The word *concussion* was the last thing I remember thinking before I fell into semiconsciousness.

I felt my spirit plummeting through the stages of Dante's *Inferno*. Devils were chasing me with knives and swords, bayonets and scythes. Snakes were curled around my arms, their mouths biting my neck. The Enemy himself, a pitiless beast with eyes of blazing fire, was in pursuit, looking to devour me whole.

Then suddenly there was a bright light. I felt as if I were on a conveyor belt moving me out of these stages of hell and leading me toward heaven. The light got brighter. Then there was a loud *boom!* And another *boom!*

The light flashed off and on, off and on, until I entered the source of light. I felt complete safety, complete warmth. No pain, no fear— just divine love. I smiled and said, "I love You, Father."

As soon as those words were spoken, the light went out.

Where was I?

What had happened?

CHAPTER I

ANTHONY

As A YOUNG KID I wanted to fly like Superman, so I'd put a towel around my neck and jump off the roof of my house. I thought I was indestructible. I was born with a burning desire to be a superhero.

For the longest time I thought this was confidence. Now I see it as a complex. Whatever you call it, I had a drive to be great at all things—athletics, academics, music. Everything was a competition, and I wanted to win.

My mother said that even as a baby, I was fearless. In a way, I suppose the circumstances of my life required me to be. My father left my mother, my two baby sisters, and me when I was a kid. From that moment I decided I would be my mom's protector and my family's savior.

We were dirt poor, living in a tiny two-bedroom, one-bathroom house in a low-income community. Like everyone else in our neighborhood, we lived off food stamps. I was going to save my family from poverty.

I remember when I was only about six years old and we were all in bed—Mom, my sisters, and I—and Mom started to cry.

"What's wrong?" I asked.

"I don't know how we're going to pay our utility bills," she said.

I stood up on the bed and made a declaration: "When I grow up, I'm going to be bigger than Elvis and pay all the bills and buy you a fancy house and a fancy car. I'm also going to become president of the United States like President Reagan."

"You can't be both," Mom told me.

"Yes, I can. I'll be Elvis during the week and the president on the weekends."

Mom laughed, but she saw I was serious-minded. She knew she could trust me. By age seven, I was cooking food on a stove for my two young siblings since Mom didn't get home from her job at JCPenney until 8 p.m. I loved my mother more than life itself. I'd do anything for her. I wanted to be a big boy and fix everything for her and the rest of my family.

* * *

I was born Anthony Scott Flippen on August 8, 1973, at Orlando Regional Medical Center. My biological father was Richard Flippen, whose family had emigrated from Ireland. Richard was in the printing business, and he was also a Marine. I remember him as a man's man—tall and strong, with big muscles, and very funny. Richard worked out with free weights in our carport. I wanted to be just like him, so I'd follow him around, picking up weights and saying, "I strong, Daddy."

He mentored the football players at Lake Brantley High, and he would let me watch their practices. Seeing the athletes throw and tackle, block and kick, I would constantly tell him, "I can do that. I'm tougher than that. I'm not scared, Daddy."

My memories of the man are few, but I cherish the ones I have.

For those first few years of my life, my father made me feel happy and safe.

Then came the day I was sitting in my dad's lap watching a Road Runner cartoon. Dad and I were laughing and having a great time, but I wanted to get closer to the television. So I lay on the floor, as close as I could get to the screen. At one point I turned back to my father to share another laugh and say, "Wasn't that funny, Daddy?" But he was no longer in the chair.

I ran to Mom.

"Where's Daddy?"

"He's not home."

"When's he coming home?"

"He'll be back soon, Anthony."

But he wasn't. He never came back at all.

Mom had nothing to say about Dad's disappearance. No further explanation was given.

I can't remember any fights between my parents. Mom married him when she was eighteen years old, half his age. Later I learned he had been married to someone else before Mom and had two sons. I never got to meet my half brothers. Many years later I learned that his younger son, Ricky, died after a long battle with alcohol and drugs. An overdose. For my entire life, nearly everything about my father's past was shrouded in mystery.

After Dad left, my sisters, Amanda and Amie, and I were sometimes taken to his tiny home in Clermont, Florida, not far from Orlando. We were told to watch television and not move from the couch. We watched *The Gong Show* while he and Mom talked in the bedroom with the door closed.

When it came to his interactions with me, Dad was distant. He didn't seem particularly enthusiastic about our visiting his place. He put up with us, but he didn't act like the dad I had loved or the dad who had once loved me. I never asked what happened between him and Mom. I just wanted Dad to move back home with us. He never did. Soon those infrequent visits stopped entirely, and just like that, he was out of my life.

With Dad gone and Mom working, I was unsupervised and free to roam the streets. I was a daredevil, and I wasn't afraid to try things other kids wouldn't do. I especially liked to impress the older kids. If one of the big kids wanted to break into a house but could only pry open a window slightly, he'd dare me to slip in. I was never one to pass on a dare. I'd sneak right in and open the front door for him.

At school, other kids made fun of me for not having a dad. They teased me for having to go to the school counselor twice a week for my misbehavior and my radically changing moods. Some of the bullies labeled me as one of the slow kids. I compensated by being the class clown who jumped on top of the desk and cracked jokes whenever the teacher left the room. I loved the attention. In my mind, the only way to win approval and acceptance from my classmates was by acting the fool.

Early on, there were divisions in my behavior—on one hand, the dutiful son wanting to please and protect, and on the other, the rebellious wild child. Even as a kid riding my bike to 7-Eleven to play Pac-Man, I thought I was the head of my household. This ego would haunt me throughout my life—an attitude that said, *There's nothing I can't do; there's nothing too big for me; I can be all things to all people.*

And yet, in the midst of this premature self-reliance and artificially pumped-up self-regard, I was introduced to a force far greater than myself. During this difficult period—before, during, and after my mom and dad broke up—I met God.

CHAPTER 2

ANCIENT WISDOM

THE CHURCH WAS ALWAYS part of my life. Days after my birth, Mom took me from the hospital to the church nursery. It's not a stretch to say the church helped raise me.

Mom loved Jesus with all her heart. Just as I knew my name was Anthony, I knew that God was real and that Jesus came to save me.

But the place I learned the true meaning of God wasn't the brick-and-mortar church. There was another church—one that had a majesty beyond my imagination. This was the place I actually saw God.

My grandfather—my mother's father—was Edward Davis of the Davis Cherokee Indian family from Cherokee, North Carolina. "If you're looking for wisdom, Anthony," he said to me, "look to the trees. Wisdom is in the wildflowers. If you're looking for God, you'll find Him in the wind."

Grandpa was a Christian and went to church every week, but he expressed his faith differently than most other Christians I knew. It was easier for him to see God in nature than in the walls of a building. "The wind is God's breath," he told me. "He breathes on you to calm your heart. This world is His creation. He created you in love."

I have many memories of walking with Grandpa through the Ocala National Forest near where he and Grandma lived. Grandpa always went shoeless on these walks. The only time he wore shoes was in church on Sundays—and even then he wore boots, not regular shoes. "I need to feel the dirt between my toes," he liked to say. "I need to remember that we're planted on this earth and that I'm a part of it."

I looked up to Grandpa like he was a real-life superhero. In the stories he told about himself, he always defeated the bad guy and saved the day. But he was quick to downplay himself. "I'm a working guy," he said. "I'm just a pipe fitter and a welder. A union man." In his younger days, he was one of thousands of men who constructed massive buildings in Chicago and New York City.

Grandpa Edward was six foot one, with a strong build and a dark complexion of reddish-olive skin. His eyes were piercing, and his hands were worn and strong. He taught me to do everything he did. At the age of eight, I was chopping wood right alongside him. He also took me fishing and hunting with him. We would go on his boat down the St. Johns River, looking for alligators. When we got right up on a gator, Grandpa would take out his .38 and blast it in the head. He told me he was protecting all the kids who played in the water. That night we'd eat gator meat.

"Don't kill nothing you don't intend on eating," Grandpa said. "You don't kill for sport. You kill to survive."

I was still a young boy when Grandpa retired from welding and moved to Sanford, about thirty miles east of Orlando. At night I'd help him haul trash to a pit behind his house (which was really a trailer built up on blocks) to build a fire. As he waved his hands over the flames, he'd describe the power of that blaze. "Anthony, look into the fire," he said. "Do you see God?"

Fire became an important element in my spiritual journey—a metaphor for God's power and mystery, just as significant as the stained-glass windows in the front of my mother's church.

In the evening, Grandma liked to sit on the swing of their porch and play what she called her "git-tar."

"Do you know why they call me Birdy?" Grandma asked.

"No, ma'am."

"Well, Son, that's because they say I sing pretty as a bluebird." She rocked back and forth on the swing. "But let me tell you about your grandfather. Do you know the story of how Grandpa fought a Brahma bull with his bare hands?"

"No, ma'am."

"Grandpa was rounding up the cows when Red, his biggest bull, charged full speed right toward him. Well, your grandfather never moved, never even flinched. And just when Red was about to ram him, Grandpa reared back and punched ol' Red straight in the mouth, flat-out knocking that animal to the ground." She nodded her head thoughtfully. "Yes, your grandfather is a man who stands his ground."

The ground Grandpa stood on had shifted over the years. He was born in Blountstown, Florida, in the horse-and-buggy days. Grandpa said that his Model T was the first motorcar in town. When he was old enough to get a job, he went to the big cities to work. Every year he went back to his roots, spending time at the Cherokee reservation in North Carolina, where he owned land and a cabin.

When I got to be four or five, he'd take me along. During the ten-hour trip from Florida to North Carolina, Grandpa told stories of our Indian relatives. He presented them as legends, but it was clear that he, too, was highly respected among the people there. As soon as we arrived, we were greeted as family and given elaborate headdresses.

At night we danced in front of the fire under a sky of brilliant stars. I could hear the cry of coyotes in the distance, making for an eerie backdrop. I didn't understand the Cherokee language, but I did my best to mimic the chants. I carefully studied the movements of the men dancing around the fire and learned to imitate them. I saw these men as great, heroic warriors, and I wanted to be just like them.

My head spun as we danced in circles, my heart in sync with an ancient rhythm that seemed to emanate from the center of the fire. I was an Indian warrior—just like the men dancing around the fire. Just like Grandpa.

"How could anyone say there's no God?" Grandpa asked the next morning. "Look at the mountains, the sky, the stars. The earth is shouting all around us, *There is a God!*"

Grandpa was always looking up.

"What do you see in the clouds, Anthony?" he said.

"They look like a white stallion."

"See how God paints pictures in His clouds. He does that to remind us He's there. God is always there, Anthony."

It was through Grandpa's description of God that, for the first time, I felt connected to something out of this world. I had a heavenly Father. I was His son.

* * *

My conversations with my heavenly Father began to replace the ones I couldn't have with my real father. I felt certain this heavenly Father loved me completely. Unlike my biological father, He would never leave me.

As we spent time at the Cherokee reservation, in the ancient woods and by the banks of the river, I sensed that Grandpa was at peace with God. I didn't know the word *mystical*, and Grandpa never used it. But that's what I was absorbing: his understanding of a mystical world far deeper than the material world. Grandpa pointed me toward the spiritual side of life, where the beauty of a pastel sunset was enough to excite my eyes with wonder and fill my heart with love.

I felt Grandpa's love as well as the love of my mother and the lost love of my father. And now I was beginning to grasp that God showered me with love because I was His child. Yet no matter how deeply I loved this Father God, I yearned and prayed for a human dad who could comfort me and teach me the ways of the world.

Much to my shock and delight, that father arrived when I was nine.

CHAPTER 3

ROLL TIDE

I SAW THE ARRIVAL of Steve Stapp as an answer to my prayers. He was our savior, come to rescue our family. I was sure his appearance confirmed that God loved me and listened to the longings of my heart.

"I have a man I want you to meet," my mother said to me one afternoon. We were living in our small house in Apopka, a working-class neighborhood near Orlando. Our life was quiet, the only real drama the reports sent to Mom detailing my bad behavior at school.

"Who is this guy?" I asked.

"A man I've been dating."

The statement came as a shock. I didn't know Mom had been dating. Why hadn't she told me? No man was going to marry my mom without my permission.

"What does he do?" I asked.

"He's a dentist."

"I hate the dentist."

"You'll like him," she replied.

What kid likes a dentist? And who wants a dentist dating your mom?

"He's a professional and a God-fearing man. He's coming over tonight."

Before Steve Stapp arrived, I wondered what he would look like. I pictured a short, chubby man with fat fingers and thick glasses. I imagined him arriving with his leather dentist's bag filled with drills.

I had no interest in this man. In my heart, I felt sure Mom should get back together with Dad, the big, strong Marine. Like almost all children of divorced parents, I wanted my family intact again. I wanted to reestablish the stability that had been shattered by their ruined relationship.

The doorbell rang.

"Answer the door, Anthony," Mom said. "It must be Steve."

I didn't want to answer it. I didn't want to see Steve. I didn't want to meet some dumpy dentist.

When I opened the door, though, I didn't see a dumpy dentist. I saw a man who bore a striking resemblance to Rock Hudson. He was six foot four with wavy black hair and a friendly smile.

"Well, young man," he said, "you must be Anthony."

Mom walked over and gave him a kiss on the cheek. "Meet Dr. Stapp, Anthony."

"That's okay, Lynda," he said to my mother. "He can call me Steve."

He spoke with a mellifluous voice and an easy manner. He was quiet—even a little shy. All my hostility flew out the window. I liked him immediately.

"I see you're wearing an Alabama football shirt," he said. "You like the Crimson Tide?"

"I love the Tide."

"I played for the Tide," he said.

"You did? Which sport?"

"Basketball and baseball."

"Wow."

"After college I tried out for the Pittsburgh Pirates."

"No way! You could have played pro baseball?"

I was starstruck.

Steve went on. "My dad was tailback at Alabama."

"You serious?"

"Ever hear of Bear Bryant?"

"Sure."

"They were roommates."

"Cool."

"Dad was a Navy man too," he told me.

"Were you in the Navy?"

"Air Force."

The more Steve spoke, the more my resistance melted. I didn't simply like this guy—I loved him. It had to be God who had sent him to us. Having Mom date Steve was far better than having her reconcile with Dad.

Dad had been distant; Steve was engaging. In his mild-mannered way, Steve was talking to me more in a single night than my father had spoken to me over the course of a year.

Once Steve saw I loved sports, he asked dozens of questions.

"What's your favorite?" he wanted to know.

"I love them all," I said. "Baseball, basketball, football, track."

"What's your best one?"

"I'm good at all of them."

"Can you dribble and hit a jump shot?"

"No one can guard me."

He laughed. I could tell he liked my confidence. "What position do you play in baseball, Anthony?"

"Shortstop and pitcher."

"How well do you hit?"

"I'm the best in my league."

"Do you bunt well too?"

"Yeah, but I never have to."

"And at track, are you fast?"

"The fastest kid in my school."

"Well, you know, I held the state record at Alabama for the 400. I bet I can catch you."

"You can try."

"Not now, boys," Mom said. "Dinner."

*   *   *

The next Sunday afternoon Steve came over again. As he approached the house, I looked out the window and saw that he drove a recent-model sky-blue Cadillac DeVille. We never had cars that nice in our neighborhood. Mom had a rusty old 1973 Datsun B210.

"Mom's in the kitchen," I told him when I opened the door.

"I didn't come to see Lynda," he said. "I came to see you."

He brought with him a brand-new Rawlings infielder's glove etched with the name Fernando Valenzuela. It smelled of fresh leather and felt like it belonged on my hand.

"Thank you so much!"

"Got a ball?" he asked.

"Yes. Do you have a glove?"

"The same one I used when I played at Alabama."

We went down the street to an empty lot and played catch for an hour. Steve could throw with devastating accuracy and blinding speed. He was impressed that I could handle just about anything he gave me—and that I wasn't afraid of the ball. He threw me grounders and gave me tips about how to field them. He shared advice about how to position my feet before I threw the ball to first or home. As a former major league prospect, he knew what he was doing. I dreamed of being a major leaguer myself, so I valued this one-on-one training.

I was sure this was only the beginning of my inside track to the big leagues.

After we played catch, Steve took me to McDonald's and said I could order whatever I wanted. We sat at a table by ourselves. I couldn't remember my biological father ever taking me to lunch—only Mom and Grandpa. I couldn't think of a time Dad had engaged me in a real conversation. He never asked me the kinds of questions Steve was asking.

"Do you believe in God, Anthony?"

"Yes, sir."

"I'm not surprised. Your mom said you have a heart for God. Do you believe that Jesus lived and died for our sins?"

"I do."

"So you've already accepted Jesus as your Lord and Savior?"

"I have."

"And you realize that we're all sinners and fall short of the glory of God?"

"Yes, sir."

"The only way to enter heaven is through the blood of Christ. Do you understand that?"

"I know Jesus is the Son of God. And that Jesus died on the cross so we could go to heaven."

"That's right, Son," Steve said. When he used the word *Son*, I felt a wave of warmth wash over me. I loved being called his son.

"And do you know the Bible?"

"I read it at church. I have John 3:16 memorized."

"Give it to me."

"'For God so loved the world that he gave his one and only Son, that whoever believes in him shall not perish but have eternal life.'"

"Perfect."

"I guess I know the Bible a little."

"You need to know it *a lot*."

"I like reading," I said. "I'm good at it."

"It sounds like you're good at everything, Anthony. How are you doing at school?"

"Sometimes I get in trouble," I confessed.

"What for?"

"Oh, well . . ." I hesitated. "Sometimes I forget the rules."

"But you know better."

"I do."

"I promise you, Anthony, I'll straighten you out. Now finish your Big Mac and we'll be on our way."

Driving back to our house, Steve stopped by his office.

"If you want to see where I work," he said, "you're welcome to come in and look around."

I was impressed with his degrees hanging on the walls and all the high-tech equipment.

"Don't worry," he said. "I'm not going to pull any of your teeth. Today is just for fun."

When we got back home, Mom and my younger sisters, Amanda and Amie, were waiting.

"Did you guys have a good time?" Mom asked.

"Great!" I burst out.

We sat around while Steve told us about his two daughters, Shanna and Summer, who were the same ages as Amanda and Amie—five and one. At first I was a bit confused. I didn't realize Steve had a family.

"Steve is divorced," my mother explained, seeing the bewilderment on my face.

Divorced was a word I never liked hearing. When it was applied to my mother and father, it brought me pain. Even in this context, it made me uncomfortable. Divorce meant people were being hurt— and even at my young age, I understood those people were usually children.

"Anthony, don't you have some homework to do?" Mom asked. "I don't want you monopolizing Steve's time."

"Don't worry about that, Lynda. Right now it's about time for the Cowboys-Redskins game." He turned to me. "Your mother tells me you're a big Cowboys fan. You wanna watch the game with me?"

My face lit up. I was certain now: Steve was perfect.

As we watched the game together, he pointed out the subtle strategies on offense and defense. He didn't just know baseball; he knew football too. I assumed he knew everything.

That night when I went to sleep and Mom came to tuck me in, she asked, "What do you think of Steve?"

"I love him," I said.

"So do I," Mom said. "So do I have your permission to keep seeing him?"

"As long as you bring me along."

"Deal."

"I love you so much, Mom."

"I love you too, my little gift from God."

* * *

Steve paid far more attention to me than he did to either my sisters or his daughters. That was understandable, since he so desperately wanted a son. And the more I was with him—the more sporting events he took me to, the more he told me about his athletic history, the more he looked over my homework and showed interest in everything I did—the more I realized how desperately I wanted a father.

I loved my mother and felt driven to do everything I could to care for her. But that responsibility was too much for an eight-year-old kid. My caring for her was a fantasy. Steve was a reality. It wasn't just a dream that he could care for us—he really could. And it was becoming evident that he actually cared. He came over two or three times a week just to check on me. No man except Grandpa had done that before. Steve made it clear that he was interested in the details of my life.

Naturally I was interested in the details of his life, but other than his profession and his sports career, I didn't learn much. Someone said that his first wife had been a beauty queen, Miss Georgia, and that their divorce had been marked by drama. But that was a story buried in the past. My mother and I saw Steve as our future.

Steve liked to talk about the steadiness of his hands—about how he had the strong, capable hands of a dentist. He saw himself as an artist, a craftsman. When he let me come to his office and watch him work, I focused on how his hands never shook, never faltered. He was a master at his profession, calling out instructions to his assistant, performing complex procedures with absolute precision. I saw him as incapable of making mistakes.

The first great bond between Steve and me was sports. The second was God. In a strange way, those two topics were connected in his mind.

One afternoon we were driving back from Vero Beach, where we had watched the Dodgers in spring training. I was excited to see their second baseman, Steve Sax, get Tommy Lasorda's autograph, and watch Fernando Valenzuela pitch. I was determined that one day I'd make the big leagues myself.

"There's no reason you can't," Steve said. "You have the talent and the desire. It's just a matter of work. Discipline is everything."

"Yes, sir."

"Without discipline we become too scattered to understand God's will. We have to discipline ourselves to read God's Word and learn to listen to Him. Do you listen to God?"

"I try."

"And what does He say?"

"That He loves me."

"But do you feel God's love?"

"I do. It's all around me."

"And you love God?"

I could honestly tell Steve that I loved God with all my heart. The God Grandpa had taught me about still warmed my soul. I prayed to Him, recognized His awesome might, and sensed His eternal goodness. I said these things to Steve, who turned toward me and patted my head.

"That's beautiful, Son. It's wonderful to hear a young boy so devoted to the Lord."

Steve encouraged my faith by giving me Christian cartoons—*Superbook* and *The Flying House*—that portrayed Bible characters as champions for God. I watched them religiously. He also began going to church with us at Calvary Assembly, the Pentecostal megachurch we'd been attending since I was born.

I was on fire for the Lord. I wanted to do everything I could to prove to Steve and to God that I was worthy. I would read the Bible, memorize the Bible, and become the best evangelist who ever walked the earth. I would show Steve that he wasn't wrong to put his faith in me. I would be a star on the field of sports and a star in the body of Christ. I felt God had enormous plans for me.

* * *

My love for Steve was boundless. When he told me that he'd proposed to my mother, that she'd accepted, and that I would soon become his son, I was happier than I'd been at any other moment of my life. He bought me a tux and asked me to be the ring bearer.

The minister from Calvary Assembly handled the ceremony, ensuring that God was blessing this couple, this family, and me. I felt as though, like my mom, I was marrying Steve.

He not only moved into our house, he also upgraded it. Under his supervision, our carport was turned into a master bedroom for him and Mom. The cracked yellow paint that covered the exterior was converted to antique bricks. Best of all, a section of concrete was set aside in the backyard to play basketball, and a regulation NBA hoop and backboard were installed.

The first week after the ceremony Steve and I were outside playing ball. During a break he said, "Son, I no longer want you to call me Steve. I want you to call me Dad."

"I will. I want to."

"And to make it official, I'm going to legally adopt you."

I didn't know exactly what that meant, but it sounded great. It sounded like he was asking to be my dad forever.

"Do you mind changing your last name to Stapp?"

"No, I want the same name as you."

So I became Scott Alan Stapp. Alan was Steve's middle name, and I wanted to be just like my dad. I was completely starting over—an entirely new identity. Anthony Flippen was now dead. Scott Alan Stapp, son of Dr. Steven Alan Stapp, was born.

I was born again.

CHAPTER 4

PARADOXES AND *PYROMANIA*

As I ENTERED my preteen years, I found myself in that awkward in-between stage. I was a kid who no longer wanted to be a kid. I wanted to be older, bigger, stronger. And I still wanted to be a superhero.

I related to the heroes I had met in my life: my real father, the Marine who had left mysteriously, never to return; Grandpa, a Cherokee warrior who introduced me to the God of the natural world; and now Steve, the gentleman/professional/former athlete/devoted follower of Jesus Christ who became the center of my world.

When Steve moved in, something changed—in him and in me. He sat me down a few weeks after the wedding and spoke to me in a tone I hadn't heard him use before.

I was no longer Anthony. I was Scott. And he was no longer Steve. He was Dad.

"Things are going to change around here, Scott," he said. "Your mother has told me about the reports she's gotten from school. I will not have a son who doesn't respect authority. I will not have a son who embarrasses my family name. I will not have a son who doesn't love God. Your misbehaving, talking back to the teachers, and acting out in class—all that's going to stop." He looked at me sternly. "Your mother also told me that you've been sneaking out your window at night. She said you were seen jumping from a friend's roof into his pool. And then a neighbor said you were mooning cars. You're headed to juvenile detention, young man."

My heart started racing. I was scared. I didn't want to go to jail.

"Do you love God, Scott?"

"Yes."

"You say you love God, but no one who loves God sins like this. You have disrespected me and betrayed God. You need to apologize to me and your mother and beg God to forgive you. Am I clear?"

"Yes, sir."

"You haven't had a man in the house for a long time, and you've walked all over your mother. Women are not, by nature, effective disciplinarians. They spoil and coddle their children. I'm not surprised that you went wild. But from now on, those days are over. Your mother is no longer in charge of you. I am. God said that the man is the priest and prophet of his household. I make the rules, and the rules will be obeyed. When rules are broken, you are not only disobeying me; you are disobeying God. And your punishment will be enforced."

"What kind of punishment?" I asked.

"Punishment without pain means nothing. The severity of the pain will keep you from repeating the offense. You were born a sinner, Scott, with a short-term memory problem. My discipline will help that memory problem. Your behavior will conform to what God and I both know is appropriate for a boy your age. I promise you will never forget my punishment. Because when I punish you, God is punishing you too."

I believed his every word. Steve spoke with unbending authority—no doubt God's authority. His voice was full of anger—God's anger, I was sure.

I was terribly afraid and confused. Before Steve, I'd gone to God for comfort. God was never angry. Now Steve was saying that when he was angry, God was angry. When Steve punished me, God was punishing me. Who was this angry, punishing God? How could He be the same God Grandpa had told me about?

In a moment, I entered the world of fear. I swore I'd never do anything to make Steve or God angry. I loved them. I wanted to please them. And if perfection was required to prove that love, well, I would try to be perfect.

My behavior in school did change. I could bring home nothing but an A in every subject. At home I focused on homework. Because I was afraid I'd lose my second father, I cut out the aberrant behavior. No more jumping off roofs, sneaking out the window, or mooning cars. I devoted myself to church and becoming a star student in Sunday school.

I went from watching the cartoon versions of Bible stories to reading the actual Bible. Their central characters—Abraham and Moses, Job and Jacob—were still role models to me, but I was introduced to them in the more sophisticated language of the King James Version. I could hear the poetry of the Bible and began to appreciate the complexities of its drama.

No drama captivated me more than David's. He was the shepherd, the poet, the psalmist. Like David, I had music and poetry surging through me. I had recently joined the school choir, and in my free time I began writing poems. David had a heart for God; so did I. He was a small man who defeated a giant. Small in stature as a boy, I could relate. As my life progressed, the parallels would continue, although there was no way I could have known it then.

Like David, I would spend time in a cave of sorts, depressed and alone. And while I'll never know what it's like to be crowned king, I can identify with the challenges of superstardom he faced—power, wealth, and women.

I spoke about David in my Sunday school class with what the teacher called unusual insight. I talked about how worldly lust had lured King David into sin. I analyzed the consequences of adultery—how David became both a manipulator and a murderer. Theoretically, I seemed to understand the story, but I was just mouthing words. Those concepts, which would be all too real later in my own life, had little meaning for me as a preteen.

Besides the Bible, other books introduced to me by my mother excited my imagination. I loved *Tom Sawyer* and *Huckleberry Finn*. Mark Twain became another hero—a writer who could create a world with words. I could hear his characters speaking, see them as though they were standing in front of me. I was with Huck as he floated down the river on the raft, every bit as present as I was in my Sunday school class each week. Twain wrote with a warmth and a sense of reality that made me want to be a writer.

I loved Edgar Allan Poe, too. I couldn't get enough of the rhythm of "The Raven": "Once upon a midnight dreary, while I pondered, weak and weary . . ." And I found myself magnetically drawn to the eerie mystery of "The Tell-Tale Heart."

It may have been an unusual selection for someone my age, but one of my particular favorites was Dante's *Inferno*. It was one thing to hear my preacher speak about hell until I could practically smell the smoke, but it was another to read Dante's imagery, which was crafted with such artful precision that the poem read more like a horror story than classic fourteenth-century literature.

* * *

Not only was I a precocious reader, I was also a precocious listener. I listened to music of all kinds—songs from Broadway musicals, church hymns, black gospel music by Larnelle Harris, and soul music by Otis Redding and Donny Hathaway. Even from a young age, I was being impacted by these musical influences.

But then one day I heard another kind of music, and my entire musical world was turned upside down.

A friend had come over with a record by a band from Britain called Def Leppard. I didn't understand the name, but I loved the music. On the cover, in yellow letters under a picture of a building in flames, was the title of the LP: *Pyromania*. The building was seen through the sight of a gun. The illustration intrigued me. I had to hear it.

The music inspired me. It resonated to my core. At age ten, I received all this as pure energy. Joe Elliott's in-your-face voice spoke to me. Phil Collen's screaming guitar had me screaming too.

My friend and I played "Photograph" and "Foolin'" at least ten times in a row. By the time we got to "Rock of Ages," with its line "I want rock 'n' roll. . . . Long live rock 'n' roll," we were both jumping up and down on the bed, playing air guitar before an imaginary audience of a hundred thousand screaming fans.

In the middle of the mayhem, my bedroom door flung open and Dad burst in. He stood there for a few seconds and listened.

"What's the name of that song?"

"'Rock of Ages,'" I said.

He nodded his head, took the cassette out of the little stereo player, and handed it to my friend.

"Go home," he said.

My friend took his cassette and ran out.

"'Rock of Ages,'" Dad repeated. "That's what they've done to 'Rock of Ages,' huh?"

I said nothing.

"Do you know the real lyrics of that song?" he asked.

"No, sir."

He closed his eyes and in a soft voice recited the words:

Rock of Ages, cleft for me,
Let me hide myself in Thee;

Let the water and the blood,
From Thy wounded side which flowed,
Be of sin the double cure;
Save from wrath and make me pure.

When he was through, I remained silent.

"Are those the words this band is singing?" he asked.

"No, sir."

"What are the words of their song?"

"I'm not sure."

"They're about rock and roll, aren't they?"

"I think so."

"You *think* so, or you *know* so?"

"I know so."

"And what do you think rock and roll is about?"

"Music."

"No, it's *not* about music. It is an instrument of Satan. It's the devil's music. Satan uses this music to control your mind, then your heart. Rock and roll is evil. To take a song about the blood sacrifice of Jesus and turn it into an invitation to sin is blasphemy."

"Yes, sir."

"You are forbidden to listen to such music—ever. You are forbidden to listen to it on records or on the radio. You are forbidden to go to a concert where this kind of music is played. In fact, you are forbidden to listen to any music where an electric guitar is played."

"Why is the electric guitar so bad?"

"Because it's the instrument of Satan, that's why. It's designed to deceive you, to cause you to do things you should not do. It's an instrument geared to defy the discipline you need to do God's will and God's will alone." He paused to take a breath. "In this house and in your life, there will be no electric guitars—ever. Tell me you understand."

"I do."

"Say it like you mean it."

"I mean it."

"I'm not sure you do. I don't hear any sincerity in your voice. I think you're still thinking about that music."

"I'm not."

"I don't believe you. There's only one way to get you to stop thinking about that music. I'm going to have to beat it out of you."

"It's already gone," I pleaded. "I promise."

My promise wasn't good enough. Dad got his strap, made me pull down my pants, and gave me a beating. The ritual had begun.

At the time, I thought I deserved the beating. I didn't have the intellectual maturity to challenge Dad. If he said rock and roll was evil, who was I to argue? He was a dentist. I was a kid. He was an elder in the church. I was just beginning to understand the Bible.

And even though my strong feelings for rock and roll wouldn't go away—I was excited whenever I accidentally heard it on the radio—I now saw that excitement as a sin to overcome. I hoped my spirit would stay strong and I wouldn't succumb to the world of flesh, personified by the songs I couldn't help but hear everywhere I went: Michael Jackson's "Beat It," Madonna's "Like a Virgin," David Bowie's "Let's Dance," AC/DC's "For Those about to Rock (We Salute You)."

Guilt hit me hard. I was sinning by liking rock and roll.

* * *

Dad always carefully checked all my work—especially my Sunday school writing. I'll never forget the time he challenged my use of the word *paradox*. I had just learned it and used it in a sentence: "It's a paradox that Jesus was both man and God."

"Do you know what *paradox* means?" he asked.

"A contradiction where two opposite things can both be true."

"God is never a contradiction," Dad said. "God is always the truth revealed, the great I Am."

"All I meant—"

"I don't care what you meant. God's Word is very clear—no ambiguities, no contradictions. It says what it says. When we start applying fancy literary words in an attempt to understand it, we lose the simple purity of the message. It's all there in black and white."

Black and white formed the basis of my thinking. There was no gray. Rock and roll was one thing. God was another. Rock and roll and God were incompatible.

"You have one critical choice to make in life," Dad said. "You either choose God or deny Him. If you are lukewarm, God will spew you from His mouth. The choice is clear. Are you ready to make that choice?"

I was ready. I chose God.

CHAPTER 5

THE RIGHTEOUS ROUTINE

My RELATIONSHIP with Dad had been growing more and more strained since he married Mom. But a single incident permanently tainted the chemistry between us.

I had gone to my friend Damon's house on Saturday to spend the night.

"Be home by 6 a.m. tomorrow," Dad had ordered, "so we can go to church together."

Like most kids, Damon and I stayed up late and didn't wake up until 7 a.m. I rushed to my house, but my family was gone. Damon's dad suggested I go to the beach with them since my parents had already left for church. He wasn't going to leave a young boy alone outside his house. So I left a note for my parents and went to the beach.

I arrived back home at three o'clock in the afternoon.

Dad was waiting for me.

"What happened?" he asked.

"I got here, but you were gone."

"Got here when?"

"Seven-thirty."

"You were to be here by six."

"We woke up late."

"And then you decided to go off on your own."

"Well, you and Mom were gone. Damon's dad wouldn't leave me alone. I had no choice."

"I told you to be here at six."

"Damon's parents forgot to wake us."

"It's your responsibility to do what I tell you."

"I didn't know what to do."

"Yes, you did. You deliberately broke the rules and chose to disobey."

"I—"

"God says to honor your mother and father. But you broke God's command—*my* command."

"I didn't mean to."

"Yes, you did. You chose to sin. You were born a sinner, and you had a relapse."

With my sister and my mother watching, my new father pulled down my pants and gave me a hard spanking.

On the outside, I was stoic. I held back my tears. But I was deeply humiliated by this spanking—especially since it was witnessed by the rest of my family. I was also angry because I thought the punishment was greater than the crime. Yes, I was an hour and a half late, but I wasn't trying to be openly rebellious. At the time, though, I didn't realize how serious an infraction tardiness was in Dad's eyes. Being prompt was one of his central obsessions.

That soon became clear when Dad presented us with the Timer. The Timer ruled our mornings. It was Dad's way of guaranteeing that our day would start off like clockwork.

The Timer was first set in the bathroom for five minutes, the amount of time I was given to shower and brush my teeth. The next setting was for six minutes—the time allotted for me to get dressed, gather my books, and show up at the kitchen table. If the Timer went off and I wasn't in my chair, I'd get beaten. After breakfast the Timer was set again. I had five minutes to wash, dry, and put away the breakfast dishes, then two minutes to put on my coat and get to the car, where Dad would be waiting to drive us to school. Anytime the Timer went off, indicating I was even a second late, a beating was in order. No exceptions.

In a strange way, this reliability was comforting. Dad was the most consistent person I'd ever met. The routine was ironclad. In order to avoid a beating, I did what I was told. Dad's world made sense.

But Dad's world also demanded perfection. I was expected to behave exactly right at all times. To attain this perfection, Dad withheld his trust. He not only supervised my behavior, he micromanaged every move I made. In the beginning, I appreciated his interest because I had never experienced such attention before. He went over every line of every one of my homework assignments. I rose to the top of my class and excelled in virtually every subject. Together we became a team—Steve, the perfect father; Scott, the perfect son.

But Dad also figured there were times I was listening to rock and roll, having impure thoughts, or doing wrong things behind his back. To make sure that such misbehavior did not go unpunished, he initiated a new policy.

One Monday night he asked, "Did you watch any of those TV shows I told you not to?"

"No, sir."

"Did you listen to any of that rock and roll?"

"No, sir."

"Did you skateboard in the church parking lot with the other hoodlums?"

"I didn't."

"Well, what did you do wrong?"

"Nothing."

"I don't believe you haven't sinned, Scott. From now on, you're going to get a beating every Monday night for those things you didn't get caught doing."

"But how do you know I did them?"

"Because I know. And now you will learn the consequences of sin. Now you will learn that there's nothing you can get away with."

The strangest part was that after the spanking he acted like nothing had happened. He came to my door while he was brushing his teeth and told me there was fresh popcorn in the kitchen. "Meet me in the living room. How about a little father-son time? *Monday Night Football*—let's see what Phil Simms can do against your Cowboys."

* * *

By the time I was twelve, I was actively serving the Lord.

Dad constantly reminded me, "Every day we live in spiritual warfare." So I put on the armor of God and went into battle, an evangelist-in-training. I went to malls, where I distributed pamphlets. I preached in playgrounds. I even gave sermons to my youth group at church. When the elders said I was anointed, Dad was proud. I was proud.

In the war for Christ, I wanted to be a soldier for my dad and for God. I thought saving souls was the most important job anyone could have. I started reading the Bible with even greater focus, quoting Scripture to my fellow students in an attempt to get them to see the light.

God's teachings were in my head; God's mission was in my heart. If you had driven past our home in Orlando, you might have spotted me on the lawn, stretched out flat on my back with my eyes to the heavens and a prayer on my lips. "I love You, Father God. Thank You for Jesus, for this life, for this family, for this chance to serve You."

Through all the madness and blessings in my life, that prayer is one thing that has not changed.

My place in God's program was reinforced by Dad's insistence that I was a special messenger. When I had just turned thirteen, he took me to Benny Hinn's Orlando Christian Center, not far from our house. Although I'd never doubted God, I did doubt Hinn and his charismatic healings. I had heard about how he'd wave his hand in front of dozens of followers, and suddenly they'd fall to the floor. Apparently that's how much of God's power he commanded. I suspected it was a hoax.

At Hinn's service, he called the young people forward for a blessing. One by one, each person fell to the ground the second he touched them. As he approached me, I firmly held on to the pew in front of me. I was determined not to fall. He never touched me; he just waved his hand in front of me. He stopped and asked me to step forward.

"There is an anointing on this young man," he said. "One day millions of people will hear his voice."

The next thing I knew, I was going down. When I awoke, I was in a daze—a beautiful daze. I felt cleansed, refreshed, renewed in body and spirit. I felt like my soul had been rinsed with Listerine. To this day, I can't explain what happened.

In my own church, I envied those who spoke in tongues. I was told that when you speak in tongues, the devil cannot interfere, ensuring that your prayers go directly to God. I begged God for the gift of tongues, but the gift never came. I cried over this. Something had to be wrong with me. Why else would God deny me the gift?

At a youth retreat, my friend Fred, a fellow basketball player, began spewing curses in a weird voice during praise and worship time. He was thought to be demon possessed. I freaked out and left the room. I walked down to the lake, where I cried out to God to remove my fear. I was afraid of demons, but I was also afraid of my father's God—a deity who told Dad to beat me and, if I wasn't perfect, would throw me into a lake of fire.

As I actively proselytized for Christ, I was warned that the devil was sure to attack. The threat only emboldened me to spread the Word with greater determination. I would win this spiritual war.

Like Steve, I saw my faith in distinctly athletic terms. I was excelling in sports, where victory is the only option. Similarly, I felt I had to be victorious for God. Defeat meant eternal life in hell, and I sure didn't want to go there.

Pleasing my father—both earthly father and divine Father—became my mission in life.

*   *   *

The struggle between darkness and light raged on inside me. One night, for no reason I could comprehend, the streetlight outside my window was blocked. I sensed something standing just outside; then I felt it entering my room. The air got thick, and fear washed over me like a heavy blanket. I felt myself choking. I knew my life was being threatened.

I distinctly heard a voice say, "If you don't stop doing what you're doing, I'll kill you."

I called out the name of Jesus and fought off the evil force. Screaming, I ran to my parents' room, where I banged on the door with all my might, crying for them to let me in. Dad opened the door. I told him what had happened, and he said I'd been attacked by a demonic presence. He let me sleep at the foot of their bed for the rest of that night and for the month following.

Dad ingrained in me a passage from 2 Timothy that says, "God hath not given us the spirit of fear; but of power, and of love, and of a sound mind" (1:7, KJV).

As a teenager, I thought my mind was automatically sound because it was formed around the clear division between good and evil. On Dad's insistence, I worked hard to stay in spiritual shape just as an athlete trains to remain in physical shape.

"Give God your all," Dad told me. "Put Him before anyone or anything else. There can be no compromise."

One of Dad's methods for keeping me in spiritual shape, besides the beatings, was his Scripture-based punishment. If the Timer went off before I'd brushed my teeth or cleared the dishes, Dad might say, "Give me two full pages of biblical analysis before you go to bed tonight. Read the book of Job, and tell me exactly what it means."

On the first reading, the book of Job is simple: God is testing Job's patience. But on the second and third readings, the meaning becomes more complex.

In the opening chapter Satan comes to God with a challenge. He claims that Job is a believer only because he's prosperous. Remove his prosperity, and you remove his devotion, Satan claims. Would God allow Satan to test Job by taking away his worldly things?

Yes, He allows it.

My first reaction was, *Why would God allow Satan to hurt us—His chosen people, His precious creations?*

As I wrote my analysis, a couple of thoughts came to mind. First, the story of Job is in the Old Testament. Humankind has not yet been redeemed. Jesus has not yet died on the cross, paying the price for our sins. And second, maybe Job's life should be viewed as a parable, just as later Jesus would tell parables in an effort to teach us the truth about God's love.

Job wins the first battle of the fight. In spite of the horrific losses he suffers, he doesn't curse the Lord but instead proclaims, "Naked I came from my mother's womb, and naked I will depart. The LORD gave and the LORD has taken away; may the name of the LORD be praised" (Job 1:21). Job doesn't blame God. He accepts his circumstances as God's will, a mystery beyond his comprehension. His faith is not shaken.

But Satan isn't through yet. He argues that if God were to take it to the next level and allow Job to be attacked physically, his faith would fail. "Strike his flesh and bones, and he will surely curse you to your face," Satan tells God (Job 2:5). The Lord agrees to this second test, with the proviso that, as Satan tortures him, he must spare Job's life.

Satan afflicts Job with boils and sores so severe that Job uses pieces of broken pottery to scrape the pus from his skin. Three of Job's friends arrive to discuss his plight. Each has a dialogue with Job, and Job has further discussions with God. The speeches are long and sometimes difficult to understand, but they come down to a single question: in light of having lost everything, can Job sustain his faith, or will he curse God?

At times Job's faith falters and he's sorry he was ever born. But in the end he still professes to God, "I know that you can do all things; no purpose of yours can be thwarted" (Job 42:2).

The reconciliation depicted at the end of the book is dramatic. Job holds tight to his faith in God while God comes through with a dramatic finish, restoring tenfold all Job has lost.

My conclusion was that ultimately God is just. If we maintain our faith and our loyalty to Him, no matter the suffering, He will reward us abundantly.

I wrote up my report with a deeper understanding than your average thirteen-year-old. When I handed it to Dad and watched him read over my words, I could tell he was impressed.

He didn't praise me, though. Instead, he took out a red pen and corrected my spelling and grammar.

"Make these corrections and write it over again," he said. "This time I don't want to see any mistakes."

I was hurt by his response. Despite everything that had happened between us, I still longed for his approval. At the very least I wanted to hear if my understanding of the book was on point. I was hoping to have a discussion with him so he could see me as something more than a willful child. But I did what I was told.

That's the last I heard of it until the next Sunday, when I was standing outside church and happened to overhear two older men discussing their Bible class.

"That Steve Stapp is really something," the first man said.

"Wonderful teacher," the second echoed.

"His reading of Job was brilliant, wasn't it?"

"This study guide is just great."

I politely asked one of the men if I could take a quick look at the guide.

"Sure, Son," he said.

The guide was the report I had written on Job.

On one hand, I was flattered. It was affirming to know that my biblical views were good enough to present to a class of grown-ups. But I was also angry. It felt unfair that my ideas were presented as Dad's work, not mine.

I wanted to say something to Dad about his deception, but I didn't. I knew better. I didn't want to get beaten.

The pattern continued. Time and again, my punishments took the form of scriptural analyses. Strangely, though, I began to fall in love with God's Word. I felt like God was using it to speak directly to me. Even from a young age, I believed this connection was God's special gift to me.

Dad never acknowledged my gift, and he never admitted that he was using me as a ghostwriter. I received neither credit nor praise. My reward, beyond the beauty of growing closer to God through His Word, was simply the avoidance of a beating.

In a moment of absolute honesty, Dad told me, "I may not be the best father, but I can tell you this: if you study His Word, it will never come back void."

My years of confusion and chaos were just beginning—years of unimaginable triumphs and baffling defeats—and yet Dad's statement held true. God's Word yields. God's Word teaches. God's Word truly connects us to Him.

When we take His Word to heart, stories like Job's become reflections of our own struggle to maintain our faith in God through any circumstance.

If only I could have embraced the strength of Job in the trials that lay ahead.

CHAPTER 6

SOUL

DAD MILITANTLY SUPERVISED what music I could hear. Fortunately, black gospel music was acceptable in his narrow list of approved genres.

If Def Leppard ignited my love for rock and roll, Take 6 ignited my love for soulful, beautiful harmonies. Take 6, a six-man Christian vocal group from Alabama, incorporated sophisticated jazz and rhythm-and-blues textures to their songs. The same was true for BeBe and CeCe Winans, a brother-sister duo whose scripturally based music touched my soul.

If Dad walked in my room and heard me listening to Luther Vandross singing "Power of Love/Love Power," he had no objection. In my mind, there was a divine quality in the soaring beauty of Vandross's songs. I felt God in his voice.

I had been drawn to soul culture from a young age. Before Mom married Steve, when I was still called Anthony, I'd break-dance at the mall with my best friend, an African American whose name was also

Anthony. We'd put out a hat in the hope of getting tips. We even won the school talent show one year. This was when Stevie Wonder and Paul McCartney were singing how ebony and ivory were living in perfect harmony.

I started singing in church choirs on a regular basis. I would harmonize with the African American kids, emulating their phrasing and learning their fantastic riffs. Nothing pleased me more than when they would turn to me and say, "Hey, white boy's got some soul!"

I believe I was drawn to gospel singers not only because of the power and range of their voices but also because of the faith they expressed. Their joyful music came out of a belief in a joyful God.

In their view God wasn't scornful or terrifying; He was a God of love to be celebrated. In these songs He was addressed as a friend. He was praised without restraint. When I heard Donny Hathaway sing "A Song for You" or "Someday We'll All Be Free," I felt God not as an intimidator but an emancipator.

In my own reading of the Bible, I saw that the book of Job was followed by Psalms—a book of songs and poems with a pulse I could feel. As I read the words of Psalm 111, I heard a melody:

> Great are the works of the LORD;
>> they are pondered by all who delight in them.
> Glorious and majestic are his deeds,
>> and his righteousness endures forever.
> He has caused his wonders to be remembered;
>> the LORD is gracious and compassionate. (vv. 2-4)

When I learned that David wrote his psalms as songs, I loved him even more. Psalm 108 was one of my particular favorites:

> My heart, O God, is steadfast;
>> I will sing and make music with all my soul.

Awake, harp and lyre!
    I will awaken the dawn.
I will praise you, LORD, among the nations;
    I will sing of you among the peoples.
For great is your love, higher than the heavens;
    your faithfulness reaches to the skies.
Be exalted, O God, above the heavens;
    let your glory be over all the earth. (vv. 1-5)

The other tremendous musical influence during this period was one I had to sneak by Dad. When I discovered U2's album *The Joshua Tree*, it was the only music I listened to for a year.

I felt Bono and the rest of the guys were speaking directly to me. They knew my thoughts, my emotions, my inner struggles.

Eventually Dad did find the album, but because of the title, I convinced him U2 was a Christian band. In this one instance, he didn't bother to listen.

I memorized the first two singles—"With or Without You" and "I Still Haven't Found What I'm Looking For"—and then I memorized every other song on the record. Bono reached me in a way no other singer ever had. To write those lyrics, I felt sure that we had a lot in common, that he'd lived a life similar to mine.

The band's sonic personality also impressed me. U2 was a real band, I thought. A band of brothers, a family. I wanted what they had.

You can't be a teenager in America and not learn the songs of the Beatles and the Stones. You have to love those songs, and I did. I admire them to this day. But of all the music I listened to during those formative teenage years, it was U2's undeniably spiritual voice—particularly Bono's piercing cry—that gave me hope. I thank God for their entrance into the world of popular music.

They were the first band to give me a glimpse into a world where God and rock and roll could coexist.

* * *

The paradoxes in my life prevailed, just as they did in my musical tastes. I accepted the concept of surrendering my will to God. I lived to do His work. And for the most part I bought into the idea of surrendering to my new earthly father. I desperately wanted to please him, and by pleasing him, I figured I was pleasing God as well.

But I was also a combatant. I never started fights, but I regularly found myself defending anyone who got picked on by bullies. When an injustice was being perpetrated, I couldn't look away. Maybe it was my Superman complex, but whatever it was, I threw myself into the thick of the battle. I wasn't big, but I was a tenacious scrapper. Sometimes I'd wind up the winner, and sometimes I'd get whipped, but I'd always make sure the other guy remembered me.

It was the same thing on the basketball court. I loved the game so much I played from morning until night. I went to San Leandro Park, where the slickest street hustlers played pickup games. I'd sit around and watch for hours, waiting until one of the guys dropped out so I could get into the game. What I lacked in height, I made up for in heart. Man, I was driven—determined to mix it up with the big boys. I was a slasher with a sweet jump shot, and eventually I won the respect of the older guys. Just one compliment—"Good job, little man"—would make my week.

My scrappy spirit came out not only on the playground and on the basketball court but also in the face of authority when I thought the person in charge was making no sense. A prime example occurred at the private school I began attending at age thirteen.

After I'd gone to public schools my whole life, Dad decided it was time to pull me out and enroll me in a strict Christian academy. My teacher there had methodologies that mirrored my father's. When it came to interpreting the messages of God, she was uncompromising.

Typically she would begin the day by saying, "God has told me that you need to sit still for the next two hours and pray. No talking, no moving. Just praying."

For thirteen-year-olds with excessive energy, this was torture.

"If you feel yourself wanting to get up and run outside or if your mind turns away from God, you are allowing temptation in," the teacher said. "And that's a sin."

As we prayed, she'd sit at her desk and read the Bible. When the two hours were up, she asked us to describe our prayers. All of us said the same thing: we'd prayed for the sick, for peace, for the poor.

"How many of you prayed that those with no knowledge of Christ would come to accept Him as their Lord and Savior?"

None of us raised our hands.

"Then take another half hour and pray about that single thought."

After a short break for lunch, we were back in the classroom. "You have to understand that your sins block you," she said. "They prevent you from knowing what God wants you to pray for. So I'll tell you. I'll let you know what message God is trying to convey to you. I'll do that until you have no sin in your life."

Then she'd get on one of her pet subjects. "One of the most common forms of sin is taking the Lord's name in vain. Nothing displeases Him more. He gave us the gift of language so we can speak of His glory. When we insult Him, we damn ourselves. Let me give you this example, class. Picture a man crossing a street. Say he stumbles on a stone. As he stumbles, he uses a word that demeans God. Then, before he can get out of the way, a car runs him over and he is instantly killed. What is his fate?"

No hands went up.

"Surely someone must know," the teacher said. "What about you, Scott?"

I thought about it for a moment. "He goes to heaven."

"No, he doesn't. God plunges him into hell, where for all eternity he burns in agony."

"All because he said a single curse word?" I asked.

"Sin is sin. And he did not repent."

"But what about the forgiveness part?"

"Jesus saved and forgave man when He was crucified—that is true. But He also instructed man that there is no way to God but through Him. We are to be perfect as Christ was perfect. If you do not repent of your sins, you will not go to heaven. If God just forgave you, you'd never stop sinning. You'd have no motivation to stop. God would never set up a kind of system that would actually encourage sin, would He?"

"I guess not," I said.

"You guess not or you know not?"

"I guess I know not."

The class laughed. The teacher didn't.

That night when I told Dad about the discussion in class, he took the teacher's side.

"Hell is no joke," he said. "Hell is real. There your soul is tortured forever. It's the worst thing that can happen to someone. It's God's wisdom, though, that created hell. Because God knew that mankind needed a serious determent from sin. The pleasures of sin are so great that only something like the prospect of a horrible hell will keep us from sinning." He gave me a hard look. "God's not stupid, Scott. He knows that the threat of punishment is the only way to get us to behave. You might say that my punishments are too severe too. But I model my system of punishment after God's. Proverbs 13:24 says, 'He that spareth his rod hateth his son: but he that loveth him chasteneth him.' God created hell because He loves us. If I give you hell, it's because I love you."

I had no doubt Dad loved me. I still believe that to this day. I also have no doubt that his discipline saved me—at least for as long as I lived in his house—from what might have been a downward path to lawlessness.

At the same time, however, my dreams were populated by demons that chased me through dark caves. I saw three-headed monsters with teeth like razor blades and whips made of fire. I felt the flames burning my back. I heard the screams. I'd wake up in terror, my sheets soaked in sweat.

In response, I did the only thing I knew to do: I witnessed with even more devotion. I told everyone I knew that Jesus was Lord and that without Him we are doomed. I spoke to children and adults alike. My desire was to give myself over to God completely. Often when I talked to people about Jesus, tears came to my eyes. In turn, my testimony brought tears to their eyes. I felt His grace all over me.

Yet at the same time I felt the oppressive presence of evil. One night I saw the image of that dark spirit outside my bedroom window again. Its shadow was visible beneath a streetlight. It came through the brick exterior of our house, directly into my room, and stood in front of my bed. I heard its voice: "Scott, stop talking to others about Christ, or I'll kill you."

I tried to get up, tried to flee, but I couldn't move. It was as though I were chained to the mattress. The more I struggled, the tighter the chains. I tried to cry out, but words wouldn't come. Finally, with one last burst of energy, I broke through, ran to my parents' room, and slept at the foot of their bed. The next morning, when Dad saw me there, he asked what had happened.

"The devil's spirit was after me again," I said. "I need protection."

"You have protection," Dad said. "You have me."

* * *

In some ways, Dad's consistency calmed and comforted me. Night after night he sat in his great leather recliner, his legs crossed and his glasses lowered on his nose, as he went over my homework. It didn't matter the assignment—he was always critiquing, correcting, chastising, and almost never praising the work. Often he would continue this routine while brushing his teeth. It wasn't unusual for him to brush his teeth for an hour or more at a time.

On one such evening, after he had marked up my homework with his red pen, I pointed out that the teacher's assignments involved religious readings only.

"What's wrong with that?" he asked.

"Shouldn't I be learning math? Don't I need to be reading history books?"

"Won't that be coming later in the semester?" he asked.

"I don't think so," I said. "I don't think this teacher cares about math or history."

Much to my amazement, Dad listened to me. The next day he called the school and learned that the curriculum was sadly lacking. His doubts about the school were triggered, but he still thought it was the best place for me.

As the school year went on, the teacher's religious fervor intensified. Rather than simply encouraging silent prayer, she now began each day with a service in which she spoke in tongues. At some point she began prophesying over certain students, making frightening predictions about their future. Then came the exorcising of demons from students who were supposedly possessed.

That was too much, even for my father. Deciding that the school was part of a cult, he took me out. The next thing I knew, I was being tested for admission to an elite private school, Lake Highland Preparatory. I was admitted at the beginning of ninth grade.

The summer before my freshman year, Dad got me a job working for one of his patients who was a landscaper. I got ten dollars a day and worked from 5 a.m. to 5 p.m. It was backbreaking labor, but I was excited to be saving money. I secretly thought maybe I could buy a guitar with the money I'd earn—not an electric, but an acoustic. I reasoned that Dad wouldn't see the acoustic as an instrument of the devil. It was calmer. Sometimes in our church a musician would sing a hymn accompanied by an acoustic guitar.

But at summer's end, when I asked Dad about it, he said, "No, I've already ordered what you're going to buy."

"Shouldn't that be my choice?"

"You don't have good judgment, Scott. You'd buy a guitar, not a rolltop desk."

A week later the rolltop arrived, paid for with my summer earnings.

"It's perfect for your Bible study," Dad said. "This desk is a beautiful piece of furniture—a place where you will examine the Word in greater depth. What do you think, Son?"

I thought I wanted a guitar. But it was easier to go with the program.

"It's fine," I said unenthusiastically.

As much as I was still smarting over the dream guitar, I realized a rolltop desk wasn't the worst thing in the world. Lake Highland would be far more challenging academically than the "cult school." I'd have to work hard to catch up with the other students.

"It's more than a matter of catching up," Dad told me. "Whatever they've accomplished, you need to exceed. You need to make the best grades in the school. You'll be known as a Christian, and you need to show what a Christian can do. A Christian does not accept second place. A Christian does not know defeat or despair. A Christian represents Christ and Christ's shining virtues. A Christian stands unstained, an example of God's moral perfection."

"Yes, sir." I was determined to prove myself in exactly those terms.

CHAPTER 7

HIGH SCHOOL HEROICS

As MY SISTERS and I grew older, Dad became increasingly obsessed with our teeth. The Timer, initially set for two minutes of brushing, was reset, forcing us to brush for four. After the brushing, Dad would come to inspect our teeth. He used that needlepoint instrument dentists favor—the kind that prods you and inflicts pain. If we missed a spot, we weren't told to brush again; we were spanked. For Dad, anything less than a spotless mouth of teeth meant an unclean heart.

At one point years earlier, Dad had told me that my baby teeth weren't falling out properly and he'd have to extract ten of them—all in one sitting. I wanted to ask whether that was necessary, but who was I to question a man who was both my father and a successful dentist? The process was excruciatingly painful.

After it was over, Dad said, "If you continue to brush properly, you will have healthy teeth for the rest of your life."

As I grew older, that same kind of laser precision Dad used on my teeth became increasingly prevalent in other realms—sports, music, church. And especially school.

He was right when he said I'd have to work hard to catch up with the other students at Highland Prep. In my first year, though, I was able to do just that. My grades were superb. In addition to my academics, I played on the school's baseball and basketball teams and led a morning Bible study.

I also stayed active at Calvary Assembly, where I was told I had a calling on my life to be an evangelist. Dad loved hearing that, and he continued to use my biblical commentaries, written out of punishment, to teach his own Sunday school classes.

My high school years coincided with the Ronald Reagan eighties, a time of moral renewal for a country recovering from the decadence of the sixties and seventies. I respected Reagan. I loved America and took pride in it. I saw myself as someone who could play an important role in this new era of conviction and purpose. And yet . . .

I liked Madonna. I thought she was hot. Scripturally I knew that to lust in the imagination was the same as realizing that lust. And yet I snuck glances at *Playboy*. I emulated Michael Jackson's dance moves. I thought Herbie Hancock's "Rockit" song and video were the funkiest things I'd ever seen or heard. I couldn't help but feel the fire of AC/DC.

Part of me wanted to dismiss this music that my father had censored. That would make life easier, and maybe it would stop the wars from raging in my head. I should just concentrate on the wholesome musicals being done at church. It would be less confusing to become a Ronald Reagan–styled leading man in *Oklahoma*.

But I couldn't silence the voice of Bono. He spoke to me in a way that wholesome musicals and Ronald Reagan, for all their good qualities, could not. The rhythms of rock—the poetry of rock—got through to my soul like nothing else.

*   *   *

Since I wasn't permitted to date or even go to movies, I put all my excess energy into sports, a pastime that Dad encouraged. My high school sports record was something both he and I could be proud of.

I was undersized and overdriven. By the time I was a junior, our basketball team was one of the best in Florida's Class A division. As a result, we were invited to play in the Apopka Invitational, where we faced 5A squads. Our school, with a fifty-member junior class, was going up against schools with six hundred in the junior class. We were outmatched but never intimidated. The most dramatic example was the night we played Warren Sapp.

Sapp would go on to play college football for the University of Miami and then pro ball with the Tampa Bay Buccaneers and the Oakland Raiders. He now has a reputation as one of the most feared defensive tackles in football history. As a high school basketball player, despite his huge size, he was agile and quick—an all-around amazing athlete.

Our team ran a flex offense that required constant motion and pinpoint passing. Warren read one of our plays, picked off my pass, and broke away. With my hardheaded attitude—believing no one should dunk on our team—I took off after him and was able to catch up just as he was leaving the floor to go to the hoop. I put my arms around his waist, and with me attached to his body, he made the dunk. When he came down, I was still clinging to him. We may have lost the game, but no one can say my heart wasn't in it.

Central Florida was a breeding ground for great athletes. I played against Johnny Damon—the future MLB all-star—who led the Dr. Phillips High School Panthers. I was told I had a great arm at shortstop, but Johnny was a man playing among boys. When he beat out my throw on two routine grounders, I wasn't discouraged. These setbacks only fueled my heroic ambitions. I worked harder.

On the day of our regional championship baseball game, which we played at a major league ballpark, the stands were packed. Grandma and Grandpa Stapp, my dad's parents, were there. I could see them beaming with pride. I had to have a special game.

We were up by a run in the top of the final inning of the game when I dove for a line drive and pulled a muscle on the right side of my lower back. The pain was excruciating. I couldn't bend down. I could barely run. The coach was going to take me out, but I begged him not to.

"You can't play short in your condition," he said.

"Then put me in left field. We only need one out."

Knowing that our pitcher was cruising along, and seeing my crazed determination, Coach went along with my plan.

The next runner got on base. Two on, two out. One more out and we'd be champions. Then an easy fly came heading to short left field. I just had to move up about twenty feet to make the catch. It was a routine play I could have made while goofing off. But when I started to run, my back went into spasms and I found myself immobilized.

The ball dropped in front of me.

Both runners scored, and we were now behind a run.

My teammates looked at me with expressions that said, *You just blew our entire season.*

In the bottom of the inning, it looked like we were at the end. Our first two hitters went down. We were down to our final out. The count was three and two . . . then the batter walked. The following hitter was walked intentionally so the pitcher could get to me. I loved that I was being underestimated. I thrived on being in such a storybook setting. I'd always dreamed of being in a game-winning situation like this.

I came to the plate with two on and two out. Pain was still shooting up my back, but at that point pain didn't matter. All that mattered was winning.

The pitcher was one of those flamethrowers who came in with

ninety-mile-an-hour fastballs. I didn't care. The harder he threw, the harder I was going to hit the thing. And sure enough, I did!

I connected, sending the ball sailing deep into the right-center gap. It took two hops and hit the fence some 375 feet away. Both runners scored. We won! The crowd went wild; my team went wild. And just the way I'd imagined it, they carried me off the field.

I enjoyed several such moments during my junior and senior years. I was even scouted by some top universities. Ultimately I was offered full academic scholarships rather than athletic scholarships since my GPA was so high. If the colleges offered me grants based on my grades, they could avoid depleting their athletic funds. I didn't care how they got me there; I just wanted to play.

These athletic heroics had a huge impact on my relationship with Dad. They made him proud, but I slowly realized they were also starting to worry him. He saw that my success in sports was making me extremely confident.

For a while our relationship endured, if tenuously. In the winter he took me to spring training to watch the major league teams that came to Florida, just as he'd done when I was younger. He took me to the Citrus Bowl in Orlando each year. And when athletic teams had prayer meetings, Dad would find out about them and make sure we both attended. Those were the happy moments. But the smallest thing could trigger his anger.

Once we were driving back from Fort Lauderdale, where we had watched a Grapefruit League game, and we were listening to the radio. We heard a report about an athlete who had been accused of sexually assaulting a woman.

"Terrible thing," Dad said.

I agreed.

"This society we live in treats sex like it's nothing," he continued. "Sex is something sacred, something holy."

He got no argument from me.

"Sex," Dad said, "is something a God-fearing man saves for his wife, and his wife alone. It's something that should not happen until marriage. And I presume it's something you have not experienced."

I answered truthfully. "No, I haven't."

"What about masturbation?" he asked.

I said nothing.

"It's a sin, you know."

"I know," I said.

"If you think impure thoughts, you'll go to hell."

As an adolescent in the middle of puberty, every time I felt attracted to a girl or had a thought about the mystery of the female body, I had to ask God's forgiveness and swear not to do it again. But again and again I broke those promises. I lived with tremendous guilt. I begged God to tell me what was wrong with me.

* * *

Strangely—or perhaps appropriately—it was over a game of basketball that the bond between Dad and me showed signs of cracking.

Ever since he came into my life, Dad and I had played one-on-one, and he'd always won. When I was sixteen, I was five foot six and weighed 120, while Dad was six foot four and weighed 230. Given my tenacity and hours of practice, I was getting close to beating him. He didn't like that idea. After all, as a high school senior, he had been named Mr. Basketball in the state of Alabama and had been a star player at the University of Alabama.

In this particular game he started muscling me harder and harder. In response, I crowded him closer and closer. We were playing "make it, take it," and I had just tied the score and had possession. If I scored, I would win.

Dad must have seen the writing on the wall, because he took the ball and threw it at me, striking me in the chest. Then he walked away.

We never played basketball again.

It became clear that, in a household where heroics were trumpeted as a way to honor God, there was room for only one superstar. In an attempt to maintain that role as I grew older and stronger, Dad employed even more physical force. He beat us with greater frequency. Once, when one of my sisters was in junior high, he took her to her room for a spanking that turned into something much more. It sounded like he was throwing her against the wall, and she was screaming so hysterically I became frightened for her life. I couldn't take it anymore, so I grabbed a baseball bat and busted through the door.

"Stop hitting her!" I yelled. "If you hit her again, I'll bust your head open! And if I can't do it now, I'll get you when you're asleep."

That was a turning point. That same afternoon Dad put a dead-bolt on his bedroom door. He was worried that I might do just what I said.

Another turning point came the day he had a horrible fight with Mom. Their marriage had been on the rocks for some time, and they even separated for a while. But to keep up appearances in church, we weren't allowed to say anything to anyone. We sat together in the front pew, pretending everything was fine.

Increasingly she was challenging him about the ways he dealt with us. He told her, "God has charged me to be the priest and prophet of this home. If you have a problem with that, take your business to God."

"My children *are* my business," she said.

"I'm running this household the way I see fit. And if I have to treat you like my sixth child, I will."

"Are you going to spank me like you spank them?" she asked.

"Keep talking back, and I will."

"I will not be spoken to as a child."

"Act like one, and you'll be treated like one."

And then, with all of us children watching, Dad took Mom on his lap—all five foot two and one hundred pounds of her—and spanked her. I can still hear her crying.

* * *

By the time second semester of my senior year came around, things were extremely tense at home. Dad was at odds with all his children as well as his wife. He would fly off the handle for no reason at all. His spankings became more erratic, frequent, and violent. I sensed that something bad was going to happen, and it was going to happen soon.

One day I walked in the door and he was immediately on my case. "Got your report card?" he asked.

"Yes, sir."

"Hand it over."

I gave him the slip of paper that showed my GPA.

"This says 3.5."

"Yes, sir."

"I thought I told you nothing less than 3.7 was acceptable."

"Three point five is pretty good. I was sure that the B plus in physics was going to be an A minus."

"You shouldn't be minus anything—you should be getting an A or an A plus. This shows you're sliding and have no respect for your father."

"I respect you. I'm not sliding."

"You're sliding *and* you're talking back. Proof that you have no respect."

"I wasn't talking back. I was trying to have a discussion with you."

"This is not a discussion. As long as you live in my home, you live under a dictatorship, not a democracy. I do the talking and you do the listening. So listen to this, Scott: you've disappointed me."

"Any other parent would be proud of his son!"

"What did you say, young man?"

"Any other parent would be proud. I'm playing three sports, I'm singing in the church choir, I'm writing your Sunday school lessons for you, and I'm still coming home with a 3.5 GPA. Nothing I ever do is good enough. I'm sick of this."

Dad's eyes turned a crazy red, and before I could react, he had me in a headlock. He managed to throw me over his knee and spanked me as if I were a child. When I got loose, he leaped at me and threw me to the floor. I was on my back and couldn't get out of the way before he started pummeling me in my stomach and my ribs.

"You think you're a man?" he yelled. "I'll show you a man!" Seeing that Dad was on the verge of doing permanent damage, Mom screamed for him to stop. When he wouldn't, she tried to get him off me. His response was to whack her in the mouth, chipping one of her teeth and busting her lip.

I finally freed myself. I was a mess—my ribs were bruised, my gut was sore. Mom was a mess too, with blood gushing from her mouth.

I looked Dad in the eye. A thousand curses came to mind, but the only words out of my mouth were, "This is it. This is the end."

CHAPTER 8

ON MY OWN

WHEN I WAS A JUNIOR in high school, I inherited my mom's old 1973 Datsun B210. Compared to the BMWs, Mercedes, and Ferraris of the kids who went to Lake Highland Prep, it was a rusty piece of junk. The front floorboards had holes in them, and I could see the pavement when I drove.

On one hand, it was completely humiliating. The kids never stopped teasing me about it. On the other hand, I felt lucky to have a car. Driving to school and church gave me my first taste of freedom. I could listen to whatever music I wanted to without fear. For the first time outside of sports, I felt connected to the other kids at school.

On a beautiful night in November 1990, with a bright full moon in the sky, that car became my escape to the world outside Steve Stapp and his God.

It was like a scene out of a movie: I slipped out my bedroom window, snuck around the house, and slowly opened the driver's side door of my Datsun. I put my keys in the ignition, pushed down the clutch, and let the car roll down the driveway. When the car reached the street, I gently pressed the brake, not wanting to make any noise.

Then I jumped out, leaving the door open, and began to push. I was thinking of the biblical character Samson, asking God to give me strength. When I pushed the Datsun to the end of the street, I jumped in and cranked it up. I was gone. I would no longer take the abuse.

I drove straight to the house of Kevin Malone, my best friend and one of the other players on the Lake Highland Prep baseball team.

I tapped on his bedroom window and woke him up.

"Dude, what are you doing here? It's three in the morning."

"I ran away from home. I need a place to stay."

He let me in and I stayed the night. In the morning I spoke with his dad, who was a successful defense attorney in Orlando.

"Scott, you're a minor, and legally I'm supposed to call your father and the local police and have them take you home," Mr. Malone said. "What is so bad at home to make you run away? I have to know more details." He paused. "But before you speak, you should understand that Kevin has been conveying to me what you've told him about your dad since you started playing baseball back in the ninth grade. Is all that true?"

I looked him in the eye. "Yes, sir," I said. "It's all true."

I filled him in on more details of the abuse at home. I also told him that lately I had started to fear not only Dad's violence but also my increasingly aggressive response to it. Our physical encounters had become more and more vicious, resulting in serious injuries for my mother and me.

"Okay," Mr. Malone said. "I'm going to call your parents and tell them you're safe and at our house. Let's talk after baseball practice today and figure out what to do. I'll have a better idea after speaking with your dad."

I don't know what transpired during their conversation. What I do know, however, is that Mr. Malone never mentioned my father to me again. He and his wife took me in and treated me like a son. Kevin became my brother.

Running away from home was by far the most radical thing I had ever done. In the conservative church world I'd been raised in, no child runs away from home. If he does, the presumption is that something is wrong with the kid, not the home he's escaping.

I knew that getting out was the right thing to do. I wasn't sure, though, if I was capable of sticking to it. The "good boy" in me—the one who saw God and Dad as the same—told me that such an act of defiance would deny me a place in heaven. I was driven by intense fear—fear of my father and a growing fear of a punishing God who would send humanity to hell simply for being human. I felt guilty, ashamed, and frightened. But in that moment, my desire for survival won out. I knew I couldn't live in a house full of emotional and physical terrorism. But even after I left, the scars Dad had inflicted still haunted me—and I had a feeling they would for the rest of my life.

Periodically demons populated my dreams. I lived with the sense that I was right on the edge of falling into the bottomless pit of a fiery hell. At times I was sure God's wrath was on me. But other times I went to Him in prayer: "Father, I love You. I've always loved You. Help me to understand, teach me to grow, let me draw closer to You. Reveal Yourself to me, I beg You, Father."

I wanted a sign from heaven. I wanted a burning bush. I wanted to see an angel from heaven. I constantly begged God to turn off my bedroom light. I needed to see that He was real.

I now see that this was the beginning of my doubt.

Then there was school. What was I going to tell my teachers and coaches about my situation at home? Mr. Malone made it clear that he would have to inform Lake Highland Prep that I was living with them. It wasn't long before the principal called me into his office.

"Scott," he said, "I understand you're no longer living at home."

"Yes, sir."

"Does that mean you've run away?"

"No, sir. My parents know where I am. I'm living with Kevin Malone and his parents."

"May I ask why?"

I explained the situation in more general terms to the principal than I had to Mr. Malone. I did not use the term *physical abuse*. I didn't want the authorities to be alerted or my father to be arrested. I believe, though, that the principal read between the lines.

"I'm afraid we have a policy, Scott, that a student who has run away from home cannot remain at Lake Highland Prep."

"I understand, sir, but as I said, I don't consider it running away. My parents know where I am."

"And will they continue to pay your tuition?"

"I don't know."

"Let me take a few days and see if I can sort this out. I'll get back to you."

The next days were difficult. I didn't know if I'd be thrown out of school—and I had only one semester left before graduation. When the principal called me back to his office, I was nervous.

"The situation is complicated," he said, "because your father is not willing to pay your tuition while you are not living under his roof. At the same time, in reviewing your academic and athletic status, no one can deny you're a well-rounded student. Your baseball and basketball coaches have expressed support for you and said they hoped you'd remain on the teams. You have one of the highest GPAs in your class." He leaned back in his chair. "For those reasons, as well as my conviction that you are a young man with tremendous potential, I'm prepared to allow you to stay through graduation, but with one provision. In order to pay your tuition, you'll be required to work at school this summer."

"What will I do?"

"You will help the janitorial staff. That means mopping floors and scrubbing toilets. Are you willing to do that?"

"I am."

Living with the Malones was a turning point in my life. It was the first time in nine years that I was not under the supervision of Steve Stapp. I definitely felt liberated, but I also felt like a foreigner in a strange world. I was curious to know what this world was all about. I still clung to my faith, but I also felt the need to test the waters a bit.

Shortly after I moved in with the Malones, I went to the one and only high school party I ever attended. Some friends from my sports teams were having a party, and I told them that I wanted to have my first drink. By that point I had quite a reputation for walking the straight and narrow.

They tricked me and gave me a nonalcoholic beer. I started acting all funny, thinking I had a buzz.

"That's no buzz," a friend said. "That's you thinking you should have a buzz. We respect you, Scott, and what you do with all those Bible studies. We don't want you to drink. We respect you for not drinking."

I felt both disappointed and proud.

*　*　*

At times the freedom in my new life was overwhelming, and I felt like I needed to get away. When that happened I'd go out in nature—to a park or to the woods—and stretch out on my back. I'd look up at the sky and talk to God.

"I love You, Father," I prayed. "Show me Your will for my life. I want to do Your will."

But after a few weeks I fell into my habit of second-guessing my decisions. Was I sure I'd done the right thing by leaving home while still in high school? Suddenly I wasn't so confident. Was I glad to be out of Steve Stapp's house? I thought so. But why did I have such trouble telling my teachers and my friends that I was living with the Malones instead of my parents? The inner conflicts continued.

The rest of the semester passed uneventfully. I excelled in my final games on the basketball and baseball teams. I did well on my exams and scored high on the SAT. Part of me was basking in my newfound freedom, but in my reflective moments, I started remembering only the positive experiences under Steve Stapp. I felt unprepared for the real world, and there was something compelling about Dad's consistency and sense of order. I also struggled with guilt, thinking I was betraying my mother and my sisters by leaving them to fend for themselves.

One day after church, I saw Dad in the parking lot. He was getting in his Cadillac as I walked by.

"I miss you, Son," he said.

He sounded sincere. Something about his words got to me. And when I looked in his eyes, I saw that he looked hurt. I thought about Jesus, about forgiveness.

I went over to say hello.

"You doing okay?" he asked.

"Pretty good."

"You look worried."

I didn't reply.

"What are you doing about college?"

"Got some invitations."

"Which schools?"

"Vanderbilt, the University of Pennsylvania. And I got a scouting letter from the athletic director at Duke."

"Good schools."

"I also just found out I was accepted into the Naval Academy's Honor Program. I don't know anything about the Naval Academy except that it's prestigious."

"How did that come about?"

"I scored high on some standardized test. They came to school and talked to me. They asked if I was interested in becoming a lawyer for the Navy."

"How are you going about evaluating all these offers?" Dad asked, sounding genuinely interested.

"Well, I want to play baseball, but I also think I want to be a lawyer. All those schools are good, right?"

"Maybe this is something we need to talk about. It's a big decision, and I know something about colleges."

At that moment, I really wanted my dad's help. But I wasn't ready to move back home.

"I'd rather not talk about it with you, Dad. I need to make the decision on my own."

"You're stubborn and overconfident, Scott," he said. "You think you know it all. You don't know anything about anything. You're going to have to get seriously humbled. I just hope it doesn't cost you your life."

At that moment I felt myself breaking. After a few long seconds, I said, "I made a mistake. Will you forgive me and let me come home?"

Those were the words I knew he wanted to hear.

"Come home for Sunday dinner."

I spent the rest of the week feeling guilty and insecure. I was now sure that running away from home had been a mistake. I missed my mother's cooking. I missed sleeping in my own bed. And I had to admit that I missed my "normal" life under Steve Stapp. For some twisted reason, that now seemed like the safer option. With all that in mind, I stopped by the house the next Sunday evening.

Mom was glad to see me, but Dad was now standoffish.

"We'd love for you to come home," Mom said. "It's not the same around here without you."

"I'm sorry, Mom," I said. "I made a mistake. I don't know what I was thinking. I made a bad decision."

"You'll be able to make better decisions living here," she told me.

Dad surprised us both by saying, "Lynda, I'm not sure I want him living here."

Dad hadn't acted like this in the church parking lot. I thought he was inviting me back.

"If he wants to come back," Dad said, "he can eat here, but I don't want him sleeping in this house. He'll have to sleep on the floor in my office. There's a pullout bed I've been using and a shower in the back."

"Why are you staying in your office?" I asked.

Dad looked at Mom, and Mom looked at me. She began to say something but stopped herself. Later I learned they had separated again. But it was still a secret that he wasn't prepared to tell people at church.

I wound up sleeping on the floor of my father's office for more than a month—the same month I was making my decision about college.

It was a strange and unsettling time for me. I was trapped again—and this time I had walked into the trap. My self-doubt and insecurity resurfaced, and once again I found myself submissive to my dad's demands. I was backtracking, leaning on him in a way he relished. He saw my ignorance and my fear of the unknown, and he preyed on my weakness.

One afternoon shortly after graduation, he said, "I've looked over these offers from the Naval Academy, Vanderbilt, and the University of Pennsylvania, and they're not what you thought they were."

"I thought they're all full rides. Doesn't that mean they pay for everything?"

"No," Dad said. "You missed the fine print."

At the time I accepted his statement. It wasn't until later that I learned he was misleading me. The schools were willing to cover all the costs.

"These aren't full scholarships," he went on. "You'll have to pay tens of thousands of dollars a year. How are you going to work, play Division I baseball, and go to school at the same time? Where are you going to get the time and the money? Besides, you're going to find yourself in over your head at those schools. They're big, and you'll just be a number. You need a college that will not only cover all your expenses but also give you the support—the *Christian* support—you'll need. I've been in touch with Lee University, and they're starting a Division III baseball team."

"Washington and Lee in Virginia?"

"No, Lee in Cleveland, Tennessee. It's a Christian school, superb in all areas. Beautiful location, right in the foothills of the Appalachian Mountains. Very picturesque." He got an intense look on his face. "But most important, there will be no distractions. College is a critical time, and you don't want to fall under the influence of secular professors and Marxist views. You don't want to get mixed up in the party world. These are your educational years when you need to absorb knowledge rooted in the Word while surrounded by other students who are doing the same."

I listened to Dad. I didn't have the emotional strength to challenge him. By that time I'd lost all my self-confidence. I was defeated. I couldn't deny that Dad's decision seemed to reflect God's instructions not to be unequally yoked with nonbelievers. It made scriptural sense for me to pursue my education in a Christian environment. That environment would sustain and protect me.

Nothing could go wrong. Or so I thought.

CHAPTER 9

LOST AT LEE

Shortly before I headed to Tennessee in the fall, I paid Grandpa Edward a visit.

"College is a great thing, Anthony," he said. "I'm proud of you for getting an education. I wish I had."

"I'm a little nervous," I confessed. "I'm not really sure what to expect at college."

"Well, there's a lot of drinking that goes on," Grandpa said. "But that doesn't mean you gotta do it. Drinking can mess you up. I know. I used to be a big drinker."

"I didn't know that."

"It's something that hurt me bad. I regret it to this day. Made enough mistakes for fifty men."

"What kind of mistakes?" I asked.

"One thing I regret was using bad language when I talked about colored folk. During that time most folks did. I'm ashamed of that. I was in Florida working as a prison guard, and I called the inmates a word that I know now is wrong. When I stopped drinking, I promised

I'd never say that word again, and I never have. I did a lot of stuff I had to make amends for."

Grandpa went on to explain how, in making amends, he chose to live a life of sobriety. He began doing charitable work. He showed up at the door of folks who were in need and gave each family three grocery bags filled with fresh fruit and vegetables from his garden. If he'd just slaughtered a deer or a pig, he'd add fresh meat. If a stranger came to his door, he'd invite him into the kitchen, where he and Birdy would prepare a meal to share. And every Sunday my grandparents served dinner for neighbors in need.

"You have fun at college, Anthony," he said. "Follow your dreams, but remember not to go hog wild. Don't drink or do any of those drugs. You'll be all right. God is always with you."

* * *

Even though the majority of the students at Lee University were Christians, I had to have been the most sheltered student there. When I arrived, I had never tasted beer. I had never seen marijuana or smoked a joint. I had never kissed a girl, much less had sex. For a guy who was a jock in high school, I was a late bloomer. I studied with girls, but that was it. I was more of a brother than a boyfriend.

Something must have happened to me that summer before Lee, though, because girls started becoming interested in me in a whole new way. College was the great liberator for me—even more so than my time living with the Malones. I was finally free of my dad's supervision. I was five hundred miles from home. And I quickly discovered that the peer pressure to party, even at a Christian college, can be intense.

For all my determination to walk the straight and narrow, I was extremely curious to find out what fun college kids were having. It didn't happen right away, but by the first of November, my curiosity was at a fever pitch.

My roommate, an All-American starting point guard for Lee

University, had a big influence on me. He was a man of deep faith, and I felt lucky to be living with him. Even though he was African American and I was white, we spoke the same language. Like me, he'd grown up playing ball on the streets and singing in church.

When I played one-on-one with him, I saw that we could be more than roommates; we could be teammates. Though I was disappointed to learn that the Lee baseball program had not yet been formed, I was confident I could play Division III basketball.

Every morning I'd see my roommate on his knees, praying and reading his Bible. And he was present at every school church service, embracing the program wholeheartedly. Those services consisted of music as well as sermons by young, up-and-coming evangelists whose zeal and commitment to the letter of the law reminded me of Steve Stapp. Maybe that's why I attended only on Sundays and refused to go on Tuesdays and Thursdays, as required.

My roommate, though, was steady in his devotion. He'd warn me of the potential pitfalls of college life. He ate right, drank lots of water, and kept his body clean. He folded his clothes military style. He was smooth and always positive—a great friend.

"Stapp," he'd say, "you know you're my brother from another mother."

One thing that surprised me, though, was his liberal attitude toward his "women friends."

"How many girls have you had?" he asked.

"Well, actually . . . none."

"That's impossible."

"Why?"

"Because this is the nineties. The sexual revolution is already thirty years old. Men aren't supposed to be virgins at eighteen."

"Well, I am. Where I come from, that's a badge of honor."

"That's sad," he said. "I know some ladies at Lee who like to have a good time. You should hang out with us and see how it goes."

"I have noticed that college girls treat me differently," I admitted.

"I've heard them talking. They think you're cute."

I couldn't help my curiosity. "Who said that?"

"Two senior girls I know."

This was a new feeling. I liked it.

"They wanted to know if you'd go to Knoxville with me to hang out with them at the University of Tennessee."

"To party?"

"What else?"

I was conflicted. I wanted to go, but knew I shouldn't. I decided to do it with the weak rationale that just because they were partying didn't mean I had to party.

Later I learned that the news of my virginity had already leaked out.

When we arrived in Knoxville Friday night, we went to a party where there were kegs of beer and bottles of booze in abundance. Immediately my new friends asked me what I wanted to drink. In an effort to act like a pro, I said, "Whiskey on the rocks"—a line I must have heard in a movie. I can't remember how much I drank, but it was enough to accept an invitation from one of the senior girls to dance. As we danced and drank, my inhibitions flew out the window.

"Let's drive back to campus," she said. "I want to be with you tonight."

"Shouldn't we think about this?" I asked. "You know girls aren't allowed in the boys' dorm."

"You can sneak me through the window," she suggested.

I hesitated.

"Something wrong?" she asked.

The smell of her perfume had me dizzy. The whiskey had my head spinning. "Nothing's wrong."

"Let's go now."

I was going crazy.

On the drive back to Lee, we kissed passionately. It was the first such kiss of my life. When we arrived, we stumbled to the dorm, both of us tipsy. She waited outside while I went to my room and opened the window. She slipped right in. With a number of false starts, we found ourselves on the top bunk, where I slept. I don't remember anything else.

When I awoke in the morning, she was gone, but I saw a note on my dresser. "Congratulations, you're not a virgin anymore. Call me when you wake up." I paused to digest her words. I couldn't remember a thing. My first night of drinking had also been my first blackout.

I was frustrated that I had no memories of what had happened on the top bunk that night, but I felt that a burden had been lifted. When I found out her sorority had a bet about who would take my virginity, my ego got a boost. I was finally a member of secular college culture.

Still, I knew I had done something wrong. Even though I'd been drinking, I knew I should have resisted. But the desire to be normal—or what I imagined was normal—won out. I wanted to be something other than a sheltered, straitlaced church boy. I wanted to feel like a regular college kid, and the fact that this Christian university handpicked by Dad was offering me real-world opportunities provided an ironic rationale to do what my hormones were telling me to do.

*   *   *

In the midst of all these new experiences, my mother called from Orlando with news that shocked me to my core.

"Grandpa died," she said.

I began to shake. Rage started to grow inside me.

"How?" My teeth were clenched tight.

"He was walking through the woods and fell down. It must have been a heart attack."

Even though I could remember Grandpa saying he hoped to die in the woods, I felt betrayed by God. So in that moment of deep loss and shock, I turned on God. I slammed the phone down and bolted outside. Running down the street crying, I screamed at God, "Why? Why? How could You take him before I said goodbye? I hate You, God!"

I fell to my knees in the middle of the street and looked to the midnight sky. I couldn't stop sobbing. I couldn't stop asking why.

Grandpa was in his eighties when he passed away. He had lived a good, long life. I wasn't really grieving for him, since I knew he was with God now. I was grieving for myself.

After Grandpa had stopped working in big cities and returned to Florida, he said, "You don't need no church—no concrete, plaster, wood, or glass. You don't need no spire or paintings on the walls. You don't need no pews and choirs and organs. That's all good, don't get me wrong. But you can find God just by walking in the woods. Stand by the ocean, and you'll hear God there. Look up to the mountains, and you'll see God there. Listen to the sound of life, and you'll hear the voice of God. You don't have to be inside no building to find God. God is everywhere."

But suddenly, with Grandpa gone, I couldn't sense God anywhere. I felt cut off not only from the grandfather I loved but also from the God of love and endless grace Grandpa had introduced me to. Now there was no one to counter my stepfather's view of God. Where Grandpa had seen God as a loving Creator and Father who accepted us despite our faults—a God who wanted me to seek Him, talk to Him, and love Him—Steve Stapp saw God as the great Judge who criticized everything I did and demanded perfection.

I lost Grandpa during the second semester of my freshman year—a time when I was questioning everything Steve had taught me to believe. Now that I was living outside the reach of his control, I felt

I had to figure out who I was and what I believed. Even if it meant poor decisions, I felt I had to learn things on my own.

* * *

One of my costliest mistakes that year happened on a camping trip in the Appalachian Mountains with two friends from Lee. For the first few hours I hiked alone, still wrestling with Grandpa's death. I couldn't understand why God hadn't allowed me to tell him goodbye.

I thought back to the night of Grandpa's death, when I had used angry words with God. For the first time in weeks, I prayed for forgiveness. Almost instantly, a sense of relief washed over me. With that weight finally off my chest, I went back to camp, where my buddies had built a fire. They were sitting around smoking.

"I didn't know you smoked cigarettes," I said.

"It's not a cigarette. Have you ever smoked grass?"

"Never."

"You interested?"

I hesitated. "I guess so."

"You gonna do it?"

"No."

"How come?"

"I don't think it's right," I said.

"According to who?"

"According to God."

"God talks about not smoking pot?"

"In Matthew, Jesus says, 'Strait is the gate, and narrow is the way, which leadeth unto life, and few there be that find it.'"

"So there's no way to smoke and love God?"

"I don't want to die," I said. "I've heard you can die from doing drugs."

"Pot just relaxes you and opens your mind to new ways of thinking."

"And you black out?"

"No, man. George Washington smoked pot. He was a pot farmer."

"George Washington, the founder of our country?"

"Yep. America was founded by men who smoked marijuana."

I tried another tactic. "They say it's a gateway drug that leads to heroin."

My friend chuckled. "I've been smoking pot since the eighth grade, and I don't even know what heroin looks like. Listen, man, we've hiked five hours into the Appalachian Mountains to find this spot. If you're ever going to try it, now's the time."

I didn't respond. I just watched as the guys passed the joint between them. I quickly saw the difference it made. They got mellow and started laughing at every little thing. It wasn't like liquor, where you start slurring your words and falling down. They were still somewhat present. The pot high looked like a different experience.

"Hey, man," one of my friends said. "It's a plant. It comes from the earth. It's not gonna kill you. Looks to me like you want a hit."

I started to rationalize. *Marijuana is a plant. It's natural. It's part of nature. I love nature. I used to see God in nature. Smoking pot in the woods is like being part of nature.*

I took a hit. The world went a little fuzzy at first, but then everything came into a new focus. My head felt cloudy, with a light pressure behind my eyes. All I could think was, *How do I feel? Am I okay? Am I high?* I suddenly felt the dirt beneath my feet, even though I had my shoes on. I quickly took them off.

One of my friends said, "That's good weed, right?"

Pushing aside my anxiety, I replied, "Yeah, bro." My next thought was, *I just said "bro." I never say "bro."*

"Stapp, what are you thinking about, buddy?"

"Dude," I said, "I'm gonna walk over to the waterfall to clean up."

"Cool, man. Don't get lost."

They giggled like five-year-olds.

When I reached the water's edge, I felt compelled to take off my clothes and stand under the falls. It was the first time since Grandpa had died that I felt close to him. Before going to sleep, with this strange experience subsiding, I scribbled down my thoughts. Years later, remembering that moment, I wrote the lyrics for the Creed song "Faceless Man."

We got back to campus on Sunday. I felt guilty about having smoked the pot, and I asked God to forgive me. I felt certain He had. But there was someone else whose grace wouldn't flow so freely.

On Monday I was told to report to the dean's office. One of the guys I'd gotten stoned with was the dean's son, and I began to worry that the dean had found out. But how? His son wouldn't have told him unless someone had found pot in his room. And even if that were the case, I couldn't imagine that my friend would rat me out. After all, he was the one who talked me into smoking in the first place.

I arrived at the dean's office five minutes early. The dean was already there.

"Hi, Scott! How are you doing?" This guy spoke so smoothly he could have been a televangelist.

"Hi, sir."

"Call me Paul."

"Okay, Paul."

"You and a couple of buddies went camping this weekend, right?"

"I did."

"Riiiiight. Okay. You boys have fun up in God's beautiful country?"

"Yes, sir." I forced a smile, playing the game.

"The Lord has revealed to me that when you came back to campus you had evil spirits in you. You boys invited evil into your bodies, didn't you?"

"Excuse me, sir—Paul. I have no idea what you're talking about."

"Did you three boys smoke marijuana up in those mountains?"

"I can only speak for myself."

"Then speak for yourself. Did you smoke marijuana?"

"Yes."

"What about the other two?"

"I can only speak for myself. What I did was wrong. I prayed to God, I confessed my sins, and I believe God has forgiven me."

"Okay, good." He sighed. "Well, that's between you and our precious Savior above. But the Lord has told me to implement and enforce certain rules here at Lee University."

"I smoked a plant, like tobacco is a plant, sir."

"You know that you allowed Satan himself to possess you with that drug."

"I disagree, sir. I—"

"As a student at Lee and a supposed child of God, you are forbidden to take drugs. Wherever you go, you represent this great institution. You also represent our risen Savior. I no longer trust you to be a righteous representative. I have no choice but to expel you."

"It's the first time I'd ever tried a drug of any kind. I've taken responsibility for my actions and made a promise to God to never smoke again."

"Well, we make lots of promises to God we can't keep, Son."

"Isn't there an appeals process?" I asked.

"No. Be out of the dorm by the end of the day."

I looked at the floor. I was speechless. At that moment I realized my life in the church was officially over.

Later that day I saw my two friends on campus.

"Your dad kicked me out of school. Are you guys kicked out too?"

Both of them said no.

"What!"

"Dude, you never confess. I grew up as a preacher's kid, and now I'm the son of a preacher/dean. I learned that when I was five."

"You gotta talk to your dad for me."

"We saved our butts. And it's cool that you didn't rat us. But man, I can't believe you confessed."

I had been taught all my life to confess. Whenever I sinned, I knew that confession was the only way to receive God's grace. Now confession had gotten me kicked out of college—and in my mind, the denomination I'd been raised in.

At eighteen years old, I was not in a good place. I was furious, resentful, and bitter. I was not about to leave Lee without challenging the dean and his theology.

Later that day I went back to his office and asked for a few more minutes of his time.

"Why, sure, Scott. Come on in."

"Sir, I don't think Lee University is representing God and His Son, Jesus Christ, as we are instructed to do in the Bible."

"Son, that's a great topic for today's sermon on campus. But that has nothing to do with your expulsion. That matter is closed. Just be grateful I didn't alert the local authorities."

I left the dean's office with a broken heart. I couldn't go back to Orlando and face my family. I didn't know where to go or what to do.

That night campus security made sure I left the dorm. With my bags in hand, I started walking to the bus station. When they finally stopped watching me, I turned around and snuck into a friend's room. He let me sleep in his closet until I could plan my next move.

Another friend let me borrow his broken-down car so I could look for a job. I was broke, and I knew Dad would never send me another dime. I had to borrow a hundred bucks from Grandma Birdy to get the car going since it drank oil like gas.

I headed for Chattanooga, the next decent-sized city, about forty miles away. I found work there as a waiter at T.G.I. Friday's. That gave me some cash and two free meals a day.

Soon, though, the closet floor was breaking my back, and I decided that living in the car would be more comfortable. Each night I parked it at a rest area ten miles away from work. This went on all winter.

Finally I saved enough money to get a studio apartment, but not enough for furniture. And because I didn't have the cash for a down payment, the utility company refused to turn on the electricity, hot water, and heat. I slept on the cold floor, and I showered by jumping in and out of the freezing water. The life I'd known was gone. *I* was gone.

I still believed in God and knew I always would, but I no longer believed in the church or this university that claimed to represent Him. I was better off scrounging around Chattanooga. I wanted nothing to do with something I considered hypocritical.

I was totally alone, totally lost. And in my mind, I was walking down the road outside grace.

* * *

Being a waiter wasn't the worst thing in the world. Working the evening shift meant I could get up late and shoot hoops with the guys in the park. T.G.I. Friday's was a popular place, so business was brisk, and the tips weren't bad. I fell into a certain rhythm. I wasn't exactly building a future, but for the first time I was getting by on my own.

I'll never forget the Saturday evening when the dean, his wife, and his son and daughter walked into the restaurant and were seated in the section I was serving.

I walked over to greet them. "Hi, welcome to T.G.I. Friday's. I'm Scott. I'll be your server. Can I get you started with some mojitos or flaming Dr Peppers?"

The dean introduced me to his wife. "Scott is one of our former students at Lee," he said.

The whole family was staring at me. I felt naked. I smiled and said, "Let me start by bringing you some water. I'll be right back."

I returned with the waters. "Can I take your order?"

They wanted burgers. I served them like they owned the restaurant. I made jokes, I stroked egos, I acted like I was interested in everything they had to say. When it was time for the check, I really wanted to say, "It's on me," but I was broke.

"Thank you for your service, young man," the dean said.

"It was so nice meeting you," his wife said.

As they walked out, I finally got a smirk from the dean's son. I was relieved when they were finally gone. I went back to bus the table, where under the dean's coffee cup was a one-hundred-dollar bill.

I stuffed it in my pocket, a little perplexed. Was this guilt money? Was the dean saying that he wronged me and wanted to make up for it? Was he just being generous? I'd never know. But it certainly didn't succeed at warming my feelings toward organized religion.

It was a rough winter. Without electricity, every evening was gloomy. I didn't have much of a past to look back on, but I could see a future. Even though I was miserable in my present condition, I still believed I had a destiny to do something great.

Then at one point that winter, the management of the apartment building learned I had no utilities—and that was against the rules. I'd have to leave, they said. But where could I go? It was back to sleeping in the car and showering at the rest area.

On my last night in the apartment, I sat on the bare floor. The only illumination was moonlight streaming through the window. I looked outside and saw a row of houses on the hill. Their lights glowed. I thought about the people in those homes. They were warm. They had families. Strangely, it was at times like this that I felt compelled to pray.

"Father, I love You. I ask You to guide me. I ask You to let me feel Your Spirit. I ask You to lead me. I ask You to help me find a home."

After that I felt prompted to return to the only home I had ever known—Orlando. Not because Steve Stapp lived there—I'd never return to his home again—but because it was a place where I had many friends. I knew the territory. I liked the weather. If I was going to scuffle, scuffling in Orlando would be a lot easier than scuffling in Tennessee.

But Orlando also represented a past that had brought me to my current state of confusion. Would I find what I was looking for in Orlando? And did I, in fact, even know what I was looking for? Does any eighteen-year-old?

CHAPTER 10

DOORS OF PERCEPTION

IN LESS THAN A YEAR I'd gone from being a scholarship student with several different offers to a guy who had been expelled and was now eking out an existence at minimum-wage jobs. Where I had once been filled with optimism, I now felt cynical. My concept of Christian justice had been shattered by a college dean. My notion of a loving heavenly Father had been smashed by an abusive earthly father. I felt I had no choice but to fend for myself, spiritually and materially.

I wasn't sure where to go next, but I knew I needed to avoid Dad at all costs. He would offer me nothing but recrimination. He wasn't interested in helping me; he was eager to shame me. I felt enough humiliation on my own—I didn't need to walk into a home where shame was the primary weapon.

Eventually I talked to my lifelong best friend, Thad Thompson, who was willing to help. He said he could hide me in his room, but if his folks found out, they'd tell my dad. I said I'd take my chances.

I wound up sleeping in his closet—another closet!—crawling in his window every night and out every morning. I found a job as a cook and started to save a little money.

Despite what had happened at Lee, I hadn't given up on college. In fact, I was more determined than ever to feed my mind. I was interested in everything—literature, psychology, religion. I knew there were poets, historians, and theologians out there with the kind of knowledge I hungered for.

Just when I didn't think my back could take another night on the closet floor, my friends Derek, Todd, and Chris Lovett took me in and let me sleep on their couch. Their dad, Virgil, was a Baptist preacher—a great guy who didn't condemn me for where I'd been or what I'd done.

Back in high school I had played basketball with these guys, and now they invited me to play on their church basketball team. Virgil wanted me in church, so I began going every Sunday in addition to playing ball in the Baptist basketball league. It was helpful for me to see that not all God's representatives were full of it. Some were actually full of love.

I found employment as a ground crew worker at a golf course in Apopka. The pay wasn't great, but the benefits were—free breakfast and lunch every day. *Thank you, Jesus.*

The biggest life change for me in Orlando involved a girl. I fell for a flower child right out of the sixties—a girl who loved rock and roll. Kim became my guide through the matrix of metal and classic rock.

"Guess who's in town?" she asked one night.

"I don't know. Who?"

"Jane's Addiction."

Four hours later we were standing in front of the stage, rocking out.

"Ever heard of Danzig?" Kim asked me a few days later.

"No."

"Check out this record. They're coming to town next week."

Kim loved all kinds of rock music, and I became a fan too. She also turned me on to Faith No More, Soundgarden, and the Scorpions.

She was a rocker chick at heart, and she lived the lifestyle. Following her lead, I became a pot smoker. We were living the stoner's life. At the same time I was also living the life of a churchgoing basketball player in the Baptist league. Maybe the two didn't go together—rock and roll and the church world—but that was me.

I had moved from the military barracks of my childhood home to the imprisonment of a parochial college to the freedom of a rock-and-roll love affair. The energy of my rebellion seemed to be doubling by the day.

I couldn't get enough of the music. I had finally found what I wanted to do—listen to rock and roll, live rock and roll, play rock and roll. I liked everything about it. The screaming guitars, the piercing singers, the funky bass lines. Rock seemed like the only outlet to express everything I was feeling on the inside—love, confusion, anger, gratitude, depression, aggression, rebellion.

For my twentieth birthday my girlfriend gave me a book about The Doors. I knew Jim Morrison's name and I'd heard the song "Light My Fire" written by The Doors' guitarist Robby Krieger—but that was about all. I stayed up until 3 a.m., devouring the book in one sitting. I was drawn into Morrison's world, taken in by his mystique. He was more than a rocker; he was a poet. There was a mysterious gentleness about him that resonated with me.

When I learned that The Doors were named after Aldous Huxley's *The Doors of Perception*, I got that book as well. Huxley wrote about his experiences taking mescaline and how, in his view, drugs were a way to open the mind. The title of Huxley's book came from a line from *The Marriage of Heaven and Hell*, written by poet William Blake in the late 1700s.

That got me reading Blake, who wrote paradoxical lines that

forced me to evaluate what I believed: "The road of excess leads to the palace of wisdom" and "The tygers of wrath are wiser than the horses of instruction." Blake's words challenged me: "Without Contraries is no progression. Attraction and Repulsion, Reason and Energy, Love and Hate, are necessary to Human existence." Because I was feeling so many contradictions in my own heart, Blake's poetry cut deep.

I was naive about the drugs. I was blind to the harm; I just saw the romance of literature and music in the rock-and-roll lifestyle. I was seduced by the beautiful Bohemian glamour of Jim Morrison. When I read his line, "Each day is a drive through history," I saw that being a serious writer and a serious rocker were not incompatible goals. Like Morrison, I wanted to be both.

And then came the revelation that would change the course of my life: Jim Morrison had gone to Florida State University in Tallahassee!

Writers described the inspiration he found there, the influential books he read, the poetry he wrote. That was good enough for me. And fortunately, Florida State had the kind of tuition I might be able to afford. Florida State, the school where the great Jim Morrison had walked the halls, was calling to me.

I saw and spoke to my mother often, but only when Dad wasn't around. She didn't seem angry about my lifestyle, but I had a feeling she didn't tell her husband what I was doing. Even if she had, I wouldn't have cared. I never wanted to see him again. As I dreamed about going to Florida State, Steve Stapp was the last person I'd want to go to for advice. I remembered his final words of wisdom to me—that I should forgo Vanderbilt and Penn and choose Lee—and I got angry all over again. This time I'd make the decision for myself.

For all our common love of rock and roll, my girlfriend and I didn't last as a couple. We were free spirits who didn't want to be bound by commitment. I never regretted meeting her and all she taught me. And she gave me one gift I'll never forget: she introduced me to a new kind of rock that would forever shape my sound and style.

Once our relationship ended, I knew it was time to go to Tallahassee. But how would I get there? My part-time jobs paid little, and I had no savings. At one point I was down to two dollars. I was too proud to call Mom or Dad. In my head I kept hearing one of Dad's favorite warnings: *"You'll never be able to make it without me! Never!"*—and there was no way I would cave and admit he was right. Just as I was renewing my commitment to do things without Dad's help, I happened to spot a Seminole jai alai fronton. I went in and, without thinking, made a two-dollar bet, won, and walked out with $102. I could survive a little longer.

My body was hungry, but my mind was even hungrier—for knowledge, for college, for an education in an atmosphere where I could thrive artistically. I had to get to Tallahassee. I didn't need a car; a motorcycle would do. But that cost money and, aside from the small wad I'd just won, I was dead broke.

* * *

Pride is a funny thing. Despite the fact that at twenty-one years old I had nothing to show for myself, I had a lot of pride. I maintained this notion of myself as a self-starter, a self-made man. I was going to stand on my own two feet. And while this pride kept me from begging Steve Stapp for money, it strangely didn't preclude the possibility of going to another source: my biological father, Richard Flippen. The more I thought about that, the more sense it made.

After all, Richard had abandoned us. Once he left, I saw him no more than a dozen times. He was always pleasant toward my sisters and me, but that was it. He gave us no financial support, and after the arrival of Steve Stapp, he didn't have to. Stapp took over, became my father, and paid for my education—until I got kicked out of Lee.

My biological father had to have some feelings of guilt, I reasoned.

Even though he had left us with a small home, he must have known he had shunned his responsibility. But the real motivator in contacting him was that I didn't have nearly the amount of emotional baggage with Richard Flippen as I had with Steve Stapp. Sure, it was painful to have a father run out on me, but that was a long time ago. Unlike the man I came to call Dad, Richard had never beaten me. He hadn't beaten my mother. As far as I was concerned, Richard Flippen was someone who was safe to approach.

Through friends and relatives, I got his number and, after a deep breath, put a dime in the phone booth.

"Hello."

"Richard Flippen?"

"That's me."

"This is your son Scott. You know me as Anthony."

"Oh, Anthony. You're calling yourself Scott now. Okay. How are you?"

"I'm fine. Can I come see you?"

"Well, we could meet for coffee at IHOP," he suggested.

"When?"

"Now, if you like."

An hour later, surrounded by the scents of coffee, bacon, and maple syrup, I was sitting across from my father, the man who had abandoned me when I was five. I didn't know what to call him. "Dad" was Steve, but at that point neither of them felt especially like a father. I figured I might as well call Richard "Dad" as well.

"Hey, Anthony," he said. "You look good. I'm glad to see you, Son."

"Good to see you too . . . Dad."

He looked young and fit for his age.

"How old are you now?" he asked.

I wanted to say, "Shouldn't a father know his son's birthday?" But I didn't. "I just turned twenty-one."

"Oh, that's right—it's in August. August 10."

"August 8," I corrected.

"Right. What have you been up to?"

"It's hard to know where to start," I said.

"Try the beginning."

I didn't want to get into a long history. It was enough to say that I didn't get along with my stepfather, that we'd had a serious parting of the ways. I told the story of what had happened to me at Lee. He sympathized, saying they were wrong to throw me out, especially after I had confessed. Then I told him about my job as a cook and how I wanted to go to Florida State.

"I hear it's a great school," he said.

"It is, but I have no way to get there."

"You mean you have no car?"

"Right."

"Cars are expensive, Son."

"Motorcycles are less expensive."

He laughed. "So you've come here to ask me to give you money for a motorcycle?"

"I'd be lying if I said no."

"And I'd be lying if I said I didn't owe it to you—that and a lot more."

"So you'll do it?"

"I will. I'm sure you already have one picked out."

"There's a Honda Shadow I can get at a good price."

"And what do I get in return, boy? A handshake? A hug?"

"A handshake."

"You're tough."

We left the restaurant laughing.

CHAPTER 11

BAND OF BROTHERS

I WAS ANGRY at God.

I was riding my Honda Shadow through the pouring rain, convinced I'd never make it the five or so hours it took to get from Orlando to Tallahassee. The rain was hitting me like needles, piercing into my face, blinding my eyes.

Can't you give me a break, God? Can you just stop the rain for a little while?

The rain kept pounding, but nothing was going to stop me. Sure, I had my doubts about this next step. I hadn't gotten into FSU, but I figured I'd start at Tallahassee Community College and then transfer. I had a friend in the area who said I could crash on his couch, but beyond that I had no idea what would happen. I had enough for tuition and nothing more. And yet something inside me was compelling me to make this move. . . .

My gut said I had to finish college.

My gut said it was Florida State or die.

My gut said I was destined to be a poet or a philosopher.

My gut said I was born to form a rock band.

I figured that at FSU, musicians grew on trees. I'd have my pick of people to start a band. I felt like everything in my life had been leading up to this moment. I'd been a soloist in choirs and school plays all my life. I'd taken some piano and guitar lessons. I knew I could sing. And if the rain hadn't been slapping me in the face, I would have been singing even then.

I was crazy with desire.

I have to make this dream come true. It's my destiny.

I arrived in Tallahassee in one piece and found my buddy, who was good to his word. I loved the city immediately. It was the perfect college town—idyllic and quaint, with red brick buildings and tree-lined streets. It was the ivory tower I'd been dreaming of. I jumped directly into the spirit of liberal education. I wasn't abandoning Jesus, but I certainly abandoned what I'd been taught growing up. I was tired of guilt; I wanted to grow.

I took courses on world religion and studied Buddhism and Islam. I learned the cultural origins and theological tenets of those faiths. I read a few chapters in the Koran. Although I didn't let go of my Christian faith, these books fascinated me. I was eager to compare other beliefs with my own. I was seeking an understanding of how different people see God and how they worship. I always struggled when a preacher would say that Jews, Muslims, Hindus, and Buddhists—every last one of them, no matter how pure of heart or righteous in deed—were doomed to burn in eternal hell. I knew Jesus as a man of mercy, a God of radical love, the embodiment of grace, the living symbol of forgiveness. This was one decision I had to leave completely in His hands.

In addition to my passion for philosophy and poetry, I was also interested in finding ways to help the disenfranchised and change the world. I also loved film, law, creative writing, and psychology.

I wanted to probe the motivations of the human heart and mind. I wanted to learn about everything.

At the same time, I wanted to rock and roll in the devil's playground. I had come to Tallahassee not only to stimulate my mind but to follow in Jim Morrison's footsteps. I was hell-bent on forming a band.

It's strange how the smallest circumstances can trigger the biggest changes in your life.

During my first term I ran into a girl I knew from high school.

"Hey, Scott," she said, "I didn't know you were here. I thought you went to Penn."

"Well, you know. . . . Things didn't work out."

"I'm glad you're here. Guess who else from Lake Highland is here?"

"Who?"

"Mark Tremonti."

A bell sounded in my head, and all at once I had a flash of memory.

I thought back to the one and only party I had attended in high school—the one where I'd been given nonalcoholic beer. I remember walking around that night, talking to several friends, when I noticed this guy sitting in the yard with a guitar in his arms. I recognized him as Mark Tremonti, a junior at Lake Highland Prep.

I opened the sliding glass door and went out to say hello. He was deep in thought, playing a song I'd never heard before.

"Hey, man," I said. "I didn't know you played guitar."

"A little, yeah."

"I sing and play a bit too."

"That's cool," Mark said.

I could tell that I had interrupted him, so I decided to head inside. "Cool, man, I'll leave you alone."

"Take care, Scott."

That was the extent of our interaction in high school.

I also remembered being told that Mark had played the national anthem on his guitar from center court during the last basketball game of his senior year. The year before I had sung the national anthem in that same spot, for the same occasion.

I asked our mutual friend if she had Mark's number. She gave it to me, and I called him the next day.

"This is Scott Stapp."

"Hey, man," he said. "You going to FSU?"

"Just started at Tallahassee Community. I'm going to get my associate in arts degree there and transfer to FSU."

"Cool."

I decided not to waste any time. "I want to start a band. You interested?"

"Sure. How about we get together and jam?"

"Great."

I went to his place, where we sat in a little room with a mattress and pillows everywhere. Both of us had acoustic guitars, and we just started playing together. I sang some lyrics that came out of nowhere, and suddenly we felt something.

It was musical love at first sight.

When it comes to music, rapport can't be explained. It just is. Why a guitarist and a singer are able to strike a common chord and produce something magical is something I don't understand. He would play a riff; I would sing a phrase. That word would lead to another riff, and that riff would prompt another phrase. We were taken over by something greater than ourselves.

From that first moment we jammed together, Mark and I knew we had great chemistry. We each had what the other lacked. He had the guitar virtuosity, and I had a message I was ready to scream. There were no long analytical discussions then—or ever, for that matter—about what we were doing or why. It was all instinctive. We were prepared for the music and stories to rush through us. We had the rare blessing of being able to play and sing what we were feeling in our souls and hearing in our hearts.

There was no doubt we shared a common culture. We both loved U2. We'd been shaped by the harder-edged bands, and we were fans of metal. We were also into the classic rock geniuses—the Stones, the Beatles, Metallica, Led Zeppelin. We deeply felt the Southern rock of Creedence Clearwater Revival and Lynyrd Skynyrd. We listened to Cream. We listened to practically everything.

But there was no open discussion of what we heard, no notion of borrowing a certain sound from any band. We were young rockers in love with the power and beauty of rock and roll. In the most genuine way, we felt that, given the way we sparked each other, we might have a shot at creating something unique.

"What do you think?" I remember asking Mark after that first afternoon of jamming.

He let a few seconds pass before saying, "I think we need to find a drummer and a bass player."

I smiled, knowing that we had the basis of a band.

*   *   *

With this goal in mind, Mark and I started going to parties, each with a guitar. We'd sit around and say to someone, "Hey, say a word—give me an idea." Someone might say, "Rage"; another person might say, "Fear" or "Freedom." And just like that, Mark would start playing and I'd start singing, making up a story on the spot. I'd paint a picture with my voice and my words. Mark would paint matching pictures with his music. We wrote free-form songs for hours on end.

Once that first building block was put in place—a singer and a guitarist with strong songwriting synergy—we went looking for the missing pieces.

I put out flyers in the hallways of dorms and on bulletin boards at bars. They simply said, "Drummer Wanted for Rock Band." At that point we had no name for our band.

In one of my classes a kid came up to me and said he'd seen the flyer.

"I'm a drummer, man," he said. "I've got a drum kit."

"Cool. Can we come over and jam with you?"

"Let's do it today."

I got ahold of Mark, and that very night we played together at the drummer's apartment. He wasn't exactly Keith Moon, but he was good enough to keep time for us. During a break, he and I went outside and I was about to say, "We want you in." In fact, the first two words had already fallen out of my mouth—"We want"—when the sound of another drummer shut me up.

I opened the door and saw that Mark was jamming with another guy to Living Colour's "Cult of Personality." This drummer was tearing it up with John Bonham–like power. Mark looked at me out of the corner of his eye as if to say, *This guy's got it*. I nodded.

"Sorry," I said to the first drummer, "but I need to listen to this other guy before we make up our minds."

Fifteen minutes later, my mind was made up. Scott Phillips, whom we shortly nicknamed Flip, got the gig. He was sensational. I was drawn to his fun-loving personality. He was the kind of guy everyone wanted around—chill and full of positive energy.

That left only one missing piece—a bassist. Getting the right bass player is tricky, and we had many tryouts. Without the right bottom, no band can get to the top. The bassist also generates unexpected blasts of energy and even melody. The bass has to complement the drummer and support the lead guitarist. He rounds out the band.

We thought we had our bass man when a guy showed up to a tryout looking the part. He had waist-long black hair and loved death metal. He could rattle off a few riffs from Slayer. We thought he could add even more of a metal edge to our vibe. But when we asked him to play a gig with us, he barely touched the strings of his bass guitar. He did a great job at acting the part, but he couldn't play the part. It was our first Spinal Tap moment. The search continued.

Our search took us to a bar to hear Baby Fish Mouth, a cover band. Their overall presentation wasn't remarkable, but their bass player looked like a rock star and played with the feeling we'd been looking for.

Brian Marshall came to jam with us the next day, and we quickly discovered that he was a great musician. The problem was he already made decent money with this cover band, and we had nothing to offer except the promise of an unknown future. But I knew Brian was a true artist, and in my mind he had no business in a cover band, no matter how much he was getting paid.

It took Brian a while to commit, but the more he played with us, the more he understood that there was something special going on. When he finally said he was in, I felt justified. I wasn't surprised that he ultimately jumped at the opportunity to be in a real band.

Or at least a group of guys who hoped to someday be a real band.

Who were we, anyway? Four college guys who liked girls, beer, and weed. We had long hair and wore backward baseball caps, flip-flops, and board shorts. Mark was working as a cook at Chili's. I was a cook at Ruby Tuesday. Scott Phillips was selling razors at Remington in the mall. And Brian was finishing up his gig with the cover band. We were rock and rollers or, to be honest, rock-and-roll wannabes.

Individually each of us might have had our doubts about how good we were, but when we came together, we felt a power that was overwhelming—a power that washed over us like a storm. It changed us. It drove us. It gave us an energy we'd never known before.

What we were experiencing, of course, was the miracle of a true band—four guys who were greater together than the sum of their parts. That was something new for me. For the first time, I had a posse, a group of like-minded brothers. This was my new family, my new sports team. The same crazed passion that possessed me in the past to win basketball or baseball games was now driving me and the band. All we needed was a name.

One night when we were jamming, Mark pulled a newspaper clipping out of his wallet that said something about the abduction of a "naked toddler."

"I always thought that would be a great name for a band," he said.

We thought it was funny and teased him about it, but Mark wasn't the kind of guy who liked to be teased. Our first gig, at a club called Yanni's, was coming up, and to avoid conflict we called ourselves Naked Toddler. The name didn't go over well. Girls hated it and said it made them think of pedophilia. They had a point.

We kept thinking.

"How about Backbone?" someone suggested.

"I don't think so."

"What about Spine?"

"Even worse."

None of the major bones in the body seemed to work. So we asked Brian, who had played with a bunch of groups, to name some of his old bands. When he said, "Mattox Creed," I heard something I liked.

"What if we just call ourselves Creed?" I asked.

"Cool," Mark said.

"I like it," Flip said.

"That could work," Brian said.

At that moment, Creed was born. I wasn't thinking in terms of a religious creed. My goal was simple: to create a rock-and-roll band.

"Creed," I told them, "means something you believe in. I believe in the four of us. I believe in this band."

The dictionary defines *creed* as a system of Christian and/or other beliefs. But believe me, if any of the other guys had thought I had God in mind when the name came up, they would have shut it down—and I would have too. We didn't have the slightest intention of introducing anything spiritual into our music. Our ambition was to be a big-time rock band like Def Leppard or Metallica.

If we had any creed at that moment, it was to rock hard, plain and simple. My subconscious, however, might have been another matter. It turned out that, without my even realizing it, the things that were happening under the surface of my heart and mind would become some of the trademarks that defined us.

But all of that was still in the future. At the time it was 1994, my sophomore year. I was twenty-one, and I already had a decent list of accomplishments. I'd made it from Orlando to Tallahassee. I was taking courses I loved. I was starting to find my way. I'd discovered something I was passionate about. And most of all, I had finally formed a band.

Life was good and getting better.

CHAPTER 12

GRIP YOUR SOUL

I SOAKED UP college like a sponge. I'd take an English lit course one day and declare myself a lit major the next. I'd take psychology the next term and be so engrossed that I'd switch to a psych major. I devoured books of all kinds, and I especially loved John Steinbeck's *The Grapes of Wrath*, Khalil Gibran's *The Prophet*, and C. S. Lewis's *The Screwtape Letters*. I read Plato and Aristotle.

I also was intrigued by visual art. I saw every film made by Orson Welles, Stanley Kubrick, and Francis Ford Coppola. Ridley Scott's *Blade Runner* was a revelation. I was stunned by Salvador Dalí's surrealism. His portrait of a crucified Christ, with its brilliant cross of cubes, put Jesus in a light I had never seen before. Because I had been brought up with blinders—with such a limited perspective on God—so many of the historical concepts, poetical constructions, and artistic innovations I was learning about were thrilling to me.

I settled down with a girlfriend—another pot-smoking rocker chick. She was a student at FSU. Meanwhile, between my romantic adventures and my intellectual endeavors, the band was quickly finding its voice.

I suppose there are actually two voices coming from any band. The first is the nonverbal voice that is solely sound. You want that sound to be immediately recognizable and unique. It has everything to do with the musical conversation between the guitarist, the bassist, and the drummer. Then there is the literal voice of the band. That, of course, is the voice of the singer. Ideally, his sound meshes seamlessly with the music.

In the beginning, it was all about experimentation. Mark's playing was always strong; he's an assertive, in-your-face guitarist. With Flip and Brian backing him up, he felt even more comfortable going on his flights of rock-and-roll riffs. We encouraged everything Mark did. But what was I going to sing about?

In our live gigs we did a predictable repertoire of cover songs— Pearl Jam's "Black," Lenny Kravitz's "Are You Gonna Go My Way," Candlebox's "Far Behind," Rage Against the Machine's "Killing in the Name," and the Red Hot Chili Peppers version of "Higher Ground." Like thousands of other groups, we were a band in search of ourselves.

The search was twofold: as a band we needed to find our own sound, and I was left to search for stories. What, if anything, did we have to say?

Was it just going to be party, party, party? Or rebel, rebel, rebel? The other guys left this matter to me. Given the influences in my background—Jim Morrison, the rocker who got me to Tallahassee; John Keats, the poet who resonated most prominently in my mind; and the psalms and stories of the Bible that had filled my head since childhood—how could my writing not reflect all that?

I saw myself as a serious writer, and I still do. I couldn't approach the process any other way. Songwriting was an outlet for something real, not something forced or invented. It was genuine expression, a passion, not some commercial concoction. It's no surprise, then, that the first thing that forged our sound as a band came from a place deep in our souls.

One day we were rehearsing in the house Flip rented seven hundred yards away from the FSU football stadium. His living room, with its reverberating hardwood floors, was our designated jam space. I stood in the space that separated the living room from the kitchen. Mark was on my right, Brian was on my left, and Flip was back by the window.

Our equipment was basic. There was no PA, so I sang through Mark's amp. As a result, it was impossible for the others to hear exactly what I was singing. But on that particular day one line I sang pierced us all:

Did my message grip your soul?

The words felt right. They felt necessary. They resonated on top of Mark's riffs. I sang them over and over again:

Did my message grip your soul?
Did my message grip your soul?

The more I sang, the more urgent the message became, the truer the question felt. We must have jammed on that idea for two hours. When we finally exhausted ourselves, we didn't have to say a word. All four of us had goose bumps. It was a feeling we'd never forget. This became our litmus test for future songs—the "goose bump test." From then on, anything we wrote had to pass the test:

We knew we had something. And even though none of us said it out loud, we believed it was only a question of time before others would know it as well.

If you had looked at us in 1994, you would have seen just another college rock band. Among the four of us, Brian had the rocker look.

Flip and Mark were the pensive musicians. I was the designated talker—and also the fighter. If we went to a frat party, for example, and anyone said anything nasty about one of my bandmates, I'd be the first to defend him. It wasn't that the other three couldn't take care of themselves—they could—but they were less impulsive. I was ready to slam someone at the drop of a hat.

Not only did I feel protective of my bandmates, but I was also apt to take on guys bigger than me. If there were two bar bullies mouthing off—one my size and the other twice my size—I'd go after the big guy. I know now that in the faces of those men I saw the face of Steve Stapp. I was fighting my father.

Because I was so tenacious, I was often successful. But because I was fearless in the people I faced, there were also times I got beaten up. Either way, the other guy left the fight knowing I was a brawler.

* * *

At a time when drugs were pervasive, our intake was hardly above the norm. One night I went on an acid trip, but I didn't step out of my ego, as others claimed to do. My visions harked back to my childhood. I saw angels seated on one shoulder and devils perched on the other. The devils were screaming, and the angels were singing. The devils, with their tongues of fire, were prepared to attack the angels, and just as they did, the angels took flight.

I tried to run from the devils and catch up with the angels, but I never got very far. Sometimes I'd run into the woods, holding my Bible, chasing down the demons that were trying to destroy me and my friends. Hallucinogenic trips took me straight to the spirit world, where the relentless battle for my soul left me feeling unsettled and afraid.

I tried to be practical. I knew that being high did not help my studies or my music. My future depended on this band.

And at the moment, what our band needed was a demo. We had

started writing songs on a regular basis, and soon we'd have enough to fill a CD. Our goal was to put out our own demo album as a way to attract either a manager or a label. So we all started saving our money. After a while we got to $1,000, but we were going to need a lot more than that. At the rate we were saving, we'd never make it.

One weekend my girlfriend's parents came to visit campus and talked about an investment plan. On a piece of paper they showed me how I could take $1,000 and triple it in a month. That would bring Creed a lot closer to our goal. As the leader of the band, I saw it as my responsibility to do all I could to get that demo made. So I took the band's $1,000 and invested it.

A month later our cool grand was gone. I'd been the hapless victim of a Ponzi scheme that had collapsed. I felt like a complete idiot, especially when I had to explain to Mark, Flip, and Brian what their brilliant leader had done with our savings.

"I didn't know what I was doing," I said. "I should have done nothing."

"Well, you're going to have to do something now," Mark said.

"I will." I promised to repay the money.

By the end of the term, I was able to make up the loss with savings from my Ruby Tuesday salary.

We slogged our way through.

Meanwhile, we were living the college scene Steve had warned me about. At a party one night, a drunk frat boy pushed a girl down the stairs. Brian and I snapped and went for the guy. In an instant, the whole fraternity turned on us. One of the guys grabbed a baseball bat and swung at Brian. I blocked the swing, and in doing so, broke my arm.

I started hanging out at a club called Pot Bellies, where a number of the early nineties bands, including Soundgarden, played. One night I was there with Brian, who by then was also my roommate. In the parking lot a drunk guy accused Brian of looking at his girlfriend.

He was so abusive to Brian that finally Brian hauled off and decked him. Then three other guys came out of nowhere. Another brawl, another bloody nose, another black eye.

Did my message grip your soul?

That was the haunting refrain that kept me writing through this intense period of my life. My days were filled with intellectual stimulation in class, and almost all my other waking hours were spent jamming at Flip's house.

Mark hit all the right chords, all the right riffs.

Brian hit all the right bass lines.

Flip hit all the right beats.

But we knew it was the right stories—the stories I knew best and had lived longest—that would give this band its identity.

At first I was afraid that those stories, so deep within me, would take a long time to come out. Yet the opposite was true. After asking that question—"Did my message grip your soul?"—the answer came quickly. I was conflicted about what message to put in the songs, so I did the most honest thing I could: I wrote about that conflict.

After one all-night jam, we went over our whole list of songs and realized that Creed had an album's worth of material. We were ready to record.

But what, in essence, was that material?

It was a dance between Mark, Flip, Brian, and me. Once we all felt locked into a vibe, a Creed song was born. For years I'd been idealizing poets and philosophers and thought maybe I'd write books someday. But when I discovered that I could express my struggles, frustrations, and conversations with God through song, I found my form.

I was grateful for my bandmates, who gifted me with this kind of artistic freedom. We played with massive conviction that came from different places—for them, it was from the music and their chops;

for me, it stemmed from the music and the message. I finally had a voice against all my oppressors, an avenue for expression that enabled me to mix gentleness with explosion, power, and fight.

* * *

Telling those stories became a joyful distraction for me. Instead of listening to a lecture in class, I'd be writing lyrics. When class was over, I'd run to a pay phone and call Mark, singing to him over the line.

The song that made the most profound impact on me was the first song Mark and I wrote after "Grip Your Soul." We called it "My Own Prison."

Prison became the most significant metaphor in my creative life. It was there at the beginning of Creed, and it would prove prophetic in the decades to come.

In some ways "Grip Your Soul," the song that turned us into a band, was a prelude to "My Own Prison." I took the things that gripped my own soul and shared them in musical form. Sharing my own prisons, questioning what this life was for, and reaching to the divine to take me higher—these themes became my obsession. The passion reflected in "My Own Prison" is something we all felt together as we played this song:

> *A court is in session, a verdict is in*
> *No appeal on the docket today*
> *Just my own sin*
> *The walls are cold and pale*
> *The cage made of steel*
> *Screams fill the room*
> *Alone I drop and kneel*
>
> *Silence now the sound*
> *My breath the only motion around*

Demons cluttering around
My face showing no emotion
Shackled by my sentence
Expecting no return
Here there is no penance
My skin begins to burn

So I held my head up high
Hiding hate that burns inside
Which only fuels their selfish pride
We're all held captive out from the sun
A sun that shines on only some
We the meek are all in one

I hear a thunder in the distance
See a vision of a cross
I feel the pain that was given
On that sad day of loss
A lion roars in the darkness
Only He holds the key
A light to free me from my burden
And grant me life eternally

Should've been dead
On a Sunday morning
Banging my head
No time for mourning
Ain't got no time . . .

I cry out to God
Seeking only His decision
Gabriel stands and confirms
I've created my own prison

These lyrics sprang from my unconscious. I didn't deliberate; I didn't sit down and try to figure anything out. The words just flowed. The prison I wrote about was of my own making, not God's. And I was guilty as charged—but of what?

Looking back, it seems like the guilt I felt went all the way back to not measuring up to the God presented to me by Steve Stapp, the punishing God for whom penance was never enough. It might sound ridiculous that after all I'd been through that same false image of God was driving me to self-imprisonment, but what can I say? When those notions are beaten into a kid at a young age, they aren't easily dismissed. They dwell deep within long after the initial damage has been done.

The fact that they came out in the form of rock and roll is both logical and amazing. I say logical because the musical form is, by its very nature, rebellious. Rock is rooted in overthrowing the previous generation's rules and restrictions. And I was rebelling against the way I was raised. But it was also amazing, because in spite of this rebellion—and inherent to this rebellion—there was a confirmation of my Savior. It was the Man on the cross, the Lion of Judah, who held the key to my freedom.

But could I address the crucified Christ through my songs? Could I share my prayers in the music? And could I say all this in the form of raucous rock and roll?

I tried. And when I did, my bandmates, deep into the music, said nothing about my lyrics except, "Cool, man, I love them." I know they didn't share my spiritual conflicts—or at least they never mentioned it. When we were together, theology just wasn't a topic of conversation. I think they felt that something powerful was being communicated when we came together for each song. I believe we all felt it. Their silent support gave me the freedom to take the songs in whatever direction the Spirit was moving me.

In "Pity for a Dime," I paint a portrait of myself, a songwriter struggling with his soul:

An artificial season
Covered by summer rain
Losing all my reason
'Cause there's nothing left to blame
Shadows paint the sidewalk
A living picture in a frame
See the sea of people
All their faces look the same

The song that most clearly depicts my internal battles during that time is "Unforgiven," where I talk about losing sight of "the irony of twisted faith." Instead of *My Own Prison*, this first album could have been called *Twisted Faith*, because so many of the themes revolved around my struggle between the false faith of my childhood and my new journey toward true faith.

Step inside the light and see the fear
Of God burn inside of me
The gold was put to flame
To kill, to burn, to mold its purity

I was still afraid that God would judge me for being impure and imperfect. But I also saw that the struggles I'd experienced in my young life now had a purpose: they helped me realize that I could survive adversity with hope and purpose.

My conflicted feelings came out in a slightly different form with "In America," where I made more of a social observation. But the struggle was still the same. I wrote about America being a place where "we kill the unborn," but also a place where "we stamp our dollar 'In God We Trust.'"

What is right or wrong?
I don't know who to believe in

My soul sings a different song
In America

Mark caught the spirit of the theme in *My Own Prison* too, when he wrote an entire song, lyrics and music, on his own. He called it "Torn."

Peace is what they tell me
Love, am I unholy?
Lies are what they tell me
Despise you that control me

The peace is dead in my soul
I have blamed the reasons for
My intentions poor
Yes, I'm the one who
The only one who
Would carry on this far

Torn, I'm filthy
Born in my own misery
Stole all that you gave me
Control you claim you save me

The peace is dead in my soul
I have blamed the reasons for
My intentions poor
Yes, I'm the one who
The only one who
Would carry on this far

Peace in my head
Love in my head
Lies, lies, lies, lies in my head

The peace is dead in my soul
I have blamed the reasons for
My intentions poor
Yes, I'm the one who
The only one who
Would carry on this far

It was a fine composition, and I was grateful for the broad talent we had in our band. My hope was that Mark would continue to gain confidence in expressing his inner thoughts and feelings. We all supported each other's artistic expressions—as long as they passed the "goose bump test." I was a fan of Mark, and Mark was a fan of me. This was the spirit behind every song Creed ever recorded.

When we finalized the group of songs for the demo, to be put under the banner *My Own Prison*, we saw no problems. We were too crazed with drive and ambition to focus on anything but the creative expression that connected us with each other and with the people who listened to our music.

At the time we were successful on a local level. After more than three years in Tallahassee, we had developed a loyal and growing fan base. But that success didn't go much beyond the borders of FSU. No rock band gets anywhere without a hunger for conquering more territory, winning over more fans, and finding a major label to distribute its music. That was our immediate goal.

And because that goal was not achieved immediately, we fought all the harder.

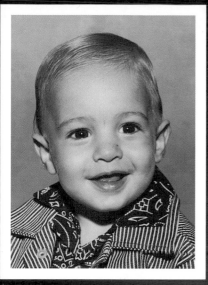

Anthony Scott Flippen at thirteen months—in my '70s zoot suit

By the time I was three, I was committed to the mullet.

And by five—enough said.

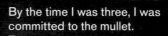

Here I am at nine, the officia[l]
man of the house, with
my mom and my two little
sisters, Amanda and Amie.

My mom, Lynda, and my
stepdad, Steven Alan Stapp

I also played basketball in high school. Of course, back then I was only five foot six, so it took a little something extra to get to the rim.

I loved playing baseball as a kid. In fact, I played all the way through high school and was scouted by a couple of college teams.

This is one of the last shots of me before I left home for college—and, ultimately, for good.

Brian Marshall, Scott Phillips, Brian Brasher, Mark Tremonti, and me in 1995, when we were still Naked Toddler

Diana and Alan Meltzer, the owners and CEOs of Wind-up, discovered us in 1997. At only five foot three, Alan looked like the Penguin from Batman, but the guy was a giant in the world of music. And I don't think anyone back then believed in us more than Diana did.

By 2001 Creed had sold more than twenty million records, and we were selling out arenas and amphitheaters all over the world.

◄ In 2002 we put on a special concert at the Winter Olympics in Salt Lake City.

Rocking out at a NASCAR event in 2010
▼

USS RONALD REAGAN
CAPT L.D. M—
COMMANDING OFFICER

▲
Playing for the troops on board the USS *Ronald Reagan* in the Gulf of Oman in 2008

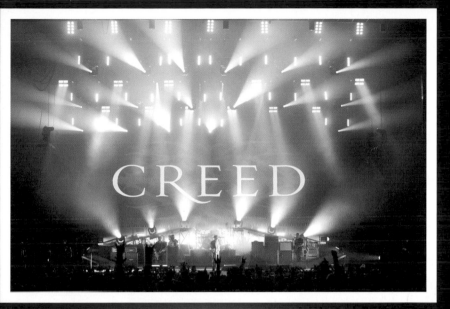

There's no way to describe the feeling you get from playing music you love in front of a live audience.

I married the love of my life, Jaclyn Nesheiwat, on February 10, 2006.

Photography by Amanda Tang

Jackie's amazing family (from left): Her sister Dina is a successful attorney; her sister Julie was awarded the Bronze Star for heroism; her sister Janette is a physician; and their mom, Hayat (seated), is an extraordinary woman and a fantastic grandma, as you can see from the expression of our daughter, Milan. Move over, Charlie—make way for Scotty's Angels.

Jaclyn and Jagger (age seven)

Jagger (eighteen months)
in the tub with Dad . . . with
arms wide open

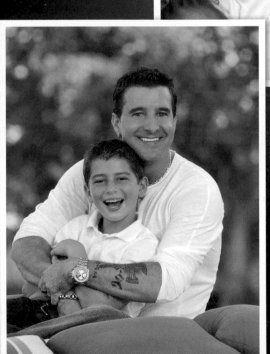

◄ At age ten, Jagger
reminds me more and more
of myself every day.

Playing with Milan (age three) in the pool

She's definitely Daddy's little girl.

With my newborn son Daniel in 2010

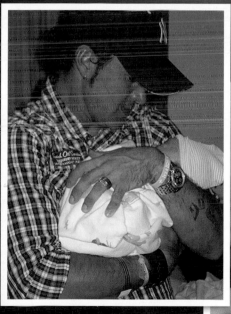

Playing with Daniel (age one) at the beach.

There was a time when Jaclyn helped me get reconnected to God. There's no question—her love saved my life.

My beautiful family. I have been blessed beyond imagination.

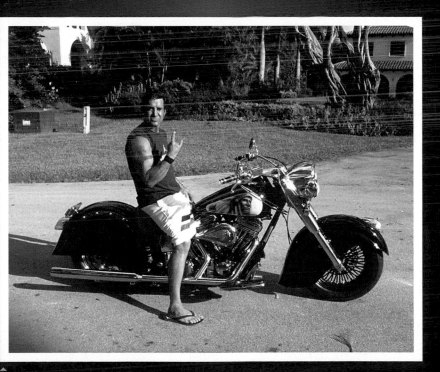

Chillin' on my Indian down in Boca.

Finally, out of the darkness and back where I belong—happy, sober

connected to God, and reunited with the band and the fans—the Reunion Tour 2012.

Giving it to God in praise. This is the only way I move forward.

CHAPTER 13

THE EINSTEIN OF
ROCK AND ROLL

IT WAS A BLOW to my ego when my girlfriend split up with me, but even at the time, I could see that maybe it was for the better. The band came first.

Creed was playing wherever we could, testing out the *Prison* material before live audiences. One Sunday we were jamming at the Mill Bakery, Eatery and Brewery for the after-church crowd—mothers and fathers, grandmothers and grandfathers, big kids and little kids. I pictured myself as a little boy in the crowd eating lunch with Mom and Dad and suddenly being assaulted by a rock band!

The main spot we played was Floyd's Music Store, where bands performed live on their stage. The owner, Jeff Hanson, became a major player in our story. After booking us at Floyd's, he became an instant believer.

Jeff's a down-home country boy—a great guy and a tireless promoter. At six foot three, he looked like Babe Ruth. Among the bands coming through Tallahassee, he was known as a tough but fair straight shooter. If he thought your band was lousy, he'd tell you to your face. If he thought you were good, he'd let you know right away.

"Look, guys," he said, "you can be the biggest rock band in the world. All you need is to be heard."

"Can you get us on the radio?" I asked.

"You need a record first."

"We haven't made one yet, but we're ready."

"That's why I want you to meet John Kurzweg."

Kurzweg was a legendary character around town. In the eighties he had a deal with Atlantic that had achieved substantial regional success. His release came around the same time as Springsteen's *Born in the U.S.A.*, when the Boss overshadowed all other rockers. John came home to Tallahassee and started playing in, recording, and producing local bands like Radio Bikini, The Front, Slapstick, Synergy, and John Kurzweg and the Night.

Because John was a preacher's kid turned rock and roller, he got me. He understood the meanings of my songs. In my eyes he was a pro with fifteen years in the business—a rock star. He was the best of both worlds: a credited songwriter as well as someone who understood my demons, choices, and struggles.

John was soft-spoken and a sensitive listener. His wild, frizzy hair gave him the look of a mad scientist. Our band saw him as the Einstein of rock and roll. He encouraged us to write more, dig even deeper, and grow as musicians. I think we paid him something ridiculous like fifty dollars a week to start the recording process. It was clear from the beginning that he was in this for the long haul.

In my opinion, John Kurzweg is the fifth member of Creed. I believe he was sent not only to guide Creed but also to mentor me during my journey. He was our angel.

* * *

John's methodology was old school. He recorded analog, direct to tape, fashioning sound in the way our ears are meant to hear it. His studio was in his home. He turned his kids' room into a vocal booth and set up the control board in a spare bedroom. I sang into a mic set up in front of bunk beds. I couldn't have cared less. I felt so lucky to be recording, I would have sung anywhere.

John produced my vocals with a firm hand, but he also had a great sense of humor. He loved to crack jokes, and he could put on a wicked British accent.

"Again," he'd say, sounding like Keith Richards. "And again."

I sang.

"Again!"

I sang again.

"And again!"

"Man, I don't think I'm ever gonna get this," I said. "Maybe I'm not feeling this today."

"Focus on your breathing. Chin down. Ooooooooopen your mouth as wide as you can. Breathe from your core, not from your chest." Then he chuckled and added, "Relax."

"John, man, it's hard to remember all that when I'm recording."

"Never stop feeling it." His voice was authoritative. "The technique will come with practice."

When I was oversinging, John was quick to say so. When I was phrasing lines in a way that felt less than natural, he had me redo the part. But he left the stories themselves alone.

John was a full-force producer. He got the best possible results out of us. If it took us fifty takes, we did fifty takes—and we didn't mind because we knew John loved the music as much as we did. He helped us realize we were better than we thought we were. He drove us in a way that inspired deeper performances than we'd ever given. He helped us express our souls in the most uncompromised and compelling form.

I was twenty-three years old. It was my senior year, and by this time I was completely committed to a career in rock and roll. All other professional notions—of becoming an author, a psychologist, a theologian, or a lawyer—were history. Creed was my life. My band-mates were my brothers. I'd take a bullet for any of them.

With the help of Jeff Hanson and his partner, Jeff Cameron, Creed now had passionate young managers, a skilled producer, and our own music. We'd had our songs mixed and mastered as professionally as the best studios in New York or LA.

We weren't going to wait around for a label to discover us. We were going to the labels themselves—not with a makeshift demo of a couple of songs, but with a complete album.

We started our own company, with our own copyrights and trade-marks, and called it Blue Collar Records. Dan Tremonti, Mark's brother, became our creative director. He was a super soulful guy with the heart and talent of a true artist. One of his photographs became the cover for *My Own Prison*. Everyone in the band loved it, though we never shared our interpretations of the piece with one another. The photo captured me to the core—it reflected the isolation, conflict, and torture that drove me. Yet in the photograph I also saw hope. I was that guy who had been beaten down but who could now get up.

We wanted the final product to be completely professional, so we hired a one-stop company to package and manufacture *My Own Prison*. We got a loan from Brian Marshall's father, who was a physician (man, we'd never loved the "good doctor" so much!). We ordered five thousand CDs.

When they arrived, we took them to the major outlets, on and off campus in Tallahassee, and asked the stores to take them on consignment. Within a month, all five thousand were sold.

Our career had begun.

* * *

One night the band was at Dan Tremonti's place. We had invited over a few FSU girls. The radio was blasting when we heard the DJ say, "There's this band around town called Creed. You know them. They've been making a lot of noise lately. They've built up quite a following, and now they've recorded their first album, *My Own Prison*. I'm guessing that right now they're sitting at home trying to impress some of their FSU lady friends. I'm gonna help them out and make their little dream come true. So, Tallahassee, here's your hometown boys—here's Creed with their radio debut, 'My Own Prison.'"

We fell down laughing but quickly told everyone to be quiet. We turned up the radio and listened like our lives depended on it. We looked at each other, stunned. Our dream was being breathed into existence.

A few days later a station in Thomasville, Georgia, began playing "Pity for a Dime," calling it their most requested song. They invited us to play at their music festival, and more than five thousand people came out for that gig.

Back in Tallahassee, we headlined at Floyd's. It seemed like the whole campus turned out. We found out later that the crowd exceeded seven thousand.

Creed was blowing up.

At a gig in Gainesville, we met Nick Ferrara, a big-time entertainment lawyer from New York with connections to the major labels. He scouted bands and got them signed. We hung on his every word.

"In the last month," Nick said, "you've sold more CDs in Tallahassee than any artist out there. The majors have taken note. They're going to be reaching out to you. But they're going to want to see you live in multiple showcases. If you can consistently do live what I hear on this CD, offers will start coming in. You're going to have to know how to play the game."

We didn't, but Nick did. And just like that, the game was on.

Enthusiasm was high. At nearly every show, it seemed like another A&R guy from a major label was in the house. Afterward they'd come backstage and congratulate us. We got nothing but compliments.

"You'll hear from us soon," the man from Sony said.

"You're amazing," the guy from RCA said.

"Deep, guys, very deep," the man from Warner said. "Here's my card."

"I want to sign you right now," the man from Atlantic said.

Nick expected a gigantic bidding war. We could only imagine the size of our signing bonus.

But then Sony passed. RCA passed. Warner passed. Only Atlantic kept calling. We were told that the top Atlantic A&R guys were crazy fans of ours. If we had a choice, we'd take Atlantic over all the others anyway. They had just signed and released Seven Mary Three, a band with connections to our hometown, and they'd told us how much they loved Atlantic. Atlantic was also the label of Ray Charles and Led Zeppelin. If Atlantic liked us, that's all we needed.

"It's going to happen," Jeff Hanson said.

"The offer will be in any day." Jeff Cameron was equally confident.

"The deal is practically done," Nick Ferrara said.

And then the deal completely fell apart. We never found out why. We weren't given any explanation. Welcome to the record business.

"Don't worry," Hanson said. "I just found out another label that's interested. The boss is coming down to see you."

"Which label?"

"Wind-up."

I'd never heard of them.

"They're new," Hanson added.

"Don't we want an established label rather than a start-up?" I asked.

"Well, so far the established labels have all passed. Besides,

Wind-up's owner and CEO, Alan Meltzer, has tons of money. He owned CD One Stop, a huge wholesale distributor, and Grass Records, a money-making label that he's turning into Wind-up."

"Well, I guess he's our only option," I conceded.

"He's also a genius," Cameron said. "He started selling records out of his house and wound up worth over a hundred million."

* * *

"You can't miss these guys," Cameron said before we went onstage for another sold-out concert in Tallahassee. "Alan Meltzer and his wife, Diana, are Mr. and Mrs. Wind-up. Alan's about five foot three, and he looks like a mafia boss. They call him the Penguin, from *Batman*. Diana used to be a model. She wears crazy hats. They both dress in black from head to toe and wear sunglasses, no matter the time of day."

Cameron was right. I couldn't miss them. They were on their feet the whole time during our show. Afterward we met them at Bullwinkle's, a local club. All of us sat at a table on the roof. I looked up, trying to soak everything in. The stars were out and the moon was full.

Diana was the first to talk. She was taller than her three-hundred-pound husband. She was shapely, and her outfit was chic. Around her waist, though, she wore a big weight lifter's belt. Adding to her bizarre look, she sported a broad-brimmed black hat with a veil, as though she were a widow in mourning.

Next to his wife, Alan looked understated in his black blazer, black slacks, and open black shirt that revealed a black silk under-shirt. He had slicked-back black hair. Like Diana, he wore huge black glasses that covered his face and prevented anyone from see-ing his eyes.

Once Diana started talking, she couldn't stop. I was pretty cer-tain I'd never heard the f-bomb so many times in one breath. "You guys are the freakin' best band I've ever heard," she said. "The minute I got your freakin' CD, I freakin' fell in love with every song. I have every last lyric memorized. They're incredible—freakin' beautiful. The world needs to hear these songs. Right? Right! Of course that's right. And that voice—that freakin' voice. That Scott Stapp. 'That guy's a superstar,' I told Alan. Scott's a Leo; Madonna's a Leo. You hear me? He's a monster, a freakin' monster! And those lyrics! I love them so much—I wrote them all down on napkins and made copies at the office and handed them out to bums in Central Park. I've been telling everyone they need to listen to this freakin' band 'cause this band is gonna save your freakin' life. They saved my life. It's like you're writing songs about my life. See, I was living in a monastery with some nuns. Don't know why I wanted to be a freakin' nun. Then I got caught doing something bad—" here she burst out laughing at herself and added, "So I said, 'Next! Next!' and I moved on. Right? Right! So here I am with you guys—Mark, with his amazing riffs, Scott Phillips, with his sexy *boom, boom*! And my sexy man Brian Marshall on the bass. You're all freakin' superstars!"

Alan took her hand, patted it, and said, "Okay, Pookie Poo, you've made your point."

"This fat guy here, Alan Meltzer, says I've got ears like a wolf. Isn't that true, Alan? Don't I have enhanced hearing?"

"She does have extra special gifted hearing," he told us in an accent that echoed Marlon Brando in *The Godfather*.

Diana went on. "Fat freakin' guy. But Alan knows music. He's made millions selling records. But me, I got the ears—I see the talent. I find the music. I love the music. And Alan? He does the business. That's nuts. I leave it to him. Don't cross this guy. If you do, you'll wind up in pieces off the Brooklyn Bridge. . . ."

Diana's monologue went on and on before Alan broke in and said it to us straight: "We want you as our first Wind-up artists. We like your music, and we think it'll sell millions of records."

"It's not about sales," Diana interrupted. "It's about love. We *love* your music. And we love this superstar, this Scott Stapp."

"Okay, Pookie Poo, that's enough."

Mark, Flip, Brian, and I sat there trying to take all this in. We had never met people like the Meltzers before.

"Are these guys for real?" I asked our manager after Alan and Diana had left.

"Is $50,000 real?" he asked. "Because that's what they're giving you to sign with their label."

With that the four of us started hugging and congratulating each other. At the time we each had about five bucks in our bank accounts. The idea of sharing $50K was insane. In addition, since Mark and I wrote the songs, he and I would split another $50,000 for Wind-up's half ownership in our publishing.

I looked up at the stars and thanked God for the chance to move into the big time. Alan and Diana Meltzer might have looked like eccentric mobsters to us, but they loved our music and were willing to pay for it.

Diana was a tragic figure, a fallen angel who, after her expulsion from the monastery, had lived her life in mourning. We loved her already. And man, did she love Creed. She showered us with gifts and art; she cooked for us; she slipped us cash when we needed it. Diana was the most hard-core fan Creed ever had. I think it's fair to say that without Diana Meltzer Creed would never have gotten out of Florida.

Immediately after our deal was signed, I left college. I was only three courses away from graduation, but rock and roll was calling.

"What's the next move?" I asked our managers.

"The road," they said in unison.

They were right. We had to bring our music to the people.

"Do we get a bus?" Flip asked.

Our managers laughed. "Try an old van and a U-Haul."

CHAPTER 14

BREAKING OUT

WELCOME TO GREENVILLE, South Carolina.

We unloaded our own equipment and set up the gear ourselves. We were our own roadies. We played at the local bar that seated a hundred. Maybe twenty people showed up. Still, we played like we were at Madison Square Garden. The applause was barely audible. We broke down our stuff, loaded it up, and moved on.

Welcome to Richmond, Virginia.

We parked in front of the club we were set to play. Across the door was a big sign that said, "Closed. Property for rent." We moved on.

Welcome to Scranton, Pennsylvania.

We were gradually starting to get a little more traction. At our first night in the local college bar that accommodated two hundred, about a hundred would-be fans showed up. A few of them had heard "My Own Prison" on the radio. Slowly our songs were filtering through. By the second night the place was nearly packed.

But later that week, when we got to New Brunswick, New Jersey, there was no buzz. The Rutgers University crowd hadn't heard of Creed yet. Again, we were playing in a practically empty bar.

None of this tainted our optimism, though, because we were barreling up the Jersey Turnpike with the Empire State Building in sight. We were about to play our first gig in New York City, and nothing could stand in our way.

Alan and Diana and a brilliant radio promo man named Bill McGathy—a stylish hippie right out of the sixties—had been hyping us like mad. We'd been told the local stations were playing us and that our arrival, even if it was in a used van pulling a U-Haul, was much anticipated.

* * *

Since hitting the road, we'd made one trip with John Kurzweg to Miami, where Wind-up paid to tweak one song and remaster the album.

"I don't want them losing any of the original energy and rawness of what we heard on that record they did themselves," Diana had told Alan. "Did I tell you these guys are the greatest rock band I've ever heard?"

"Yes, you have, Pookie Poo," he said, trying to cut her off at the pass.

"The only change this record's going to have will be the Wind-up label logo and my name as A&R chief, because I discovered this freakin' band. I brought them to you, Alan, and don't you ever forget that."

Everything was in place, and although the gigs leading up to New York had been less than spectacular, seeing that skyline across the Hudson had us feeling like Dorothy entering Oz. We were off to see the wizards who went by the names Alan and Diana Meltzer.

In New York they greeted us as conquering heroes, even though we hadn't conquered a thing. They put us up in a swank hotel and showcased us in several clubs around the city. The media came out, and so did a surprising number of new fans. The Meltzer/McGathy promo team was on fire, and the energy of the city had us playing with more passion than ever before.

If you asked me what profession requires more drive and ambition—rock and roll or politics—I'd be hard-pressed to answer. Winning over a fan base is a lot like winning an election. It requires nothing short of a rigorous day-after-day, week-after-week, month-after-month campaign. You go where you have to go to meet and rock the people.

In our case, that meant piling into the van and heading out to the great American Midwest, West, Southwest, and back home to the Southeast. We were getting some airplay and making gradual but steady progress. In the rock landscape of 1997—where The Wallflowers, U2, Matchbox Twenty, Garbage, and Smash Mouth were riding high—we were catching up.

I don't know when it happened—I can't pin it to a particular date—but late that year we went from playing bars and medium-size clubs to playing large clubs and half arenas. A full arena might hold sixteen thousand, but in our case they closed off half the space to accommodate eight thousand. We were ready for the crowds.

When we got back to Tallahassee for a brief rest after our first national tour, *My Own Prison* was climbing the national charts. After every show someone held terry-cloth robes for us to slip into like we were the Rolling Stones. Each of us had our own limo that would whisk us to a private airport. Then there was the Gulfstream V—the jet Meltzer said he'd bought for us. A gorgeous stewardess served us filet mignon, lobster, and foreign beer we couldn't even pronounce. (Years later we'd learn that not only did Meltzer keep the plane for his own use, he'd bought it with songwriting royalties that should have gone to me and Mark.)

In less than two years we'd gone from being broke stoner rockers wearing flip-flops to four guys worth millions—with hundreds of thousands coming in every day.

* * *

Years had passed since I'd spoken to Steve Stapp. When I got back to Tallahassee, I would occasionally contact my mom to make sure she was okay, but never her husband. I was still bitter. In the aftermath of my early success, I wanted to tell him that he'd been wrong when he said I would be nothing without him. Time and time again, he had predicted nothing but failure for me. He had called me a loser and a sinner unworthy of redemption. I wanted to rub my triumph in his face.

But I didn't. I knew that would be prideful, and besides, I still didn't want to see the man or even hear his voice.

I didn't adjust well to the merry-go-round of superstardom. I got dizzy and stayed dizzy for years. I didn't have the wisdom to see how an already big ego, made massive by the joyride of rock and roll, could do me in.

And it wasn't even the partying—yet. It was the false sense that I couldn't fail. That nothing could stop me, nothing could harm me. I had been Superman, the warrior for Jesus when I was a kid; I'd been the basketball champion, the academic star in high school. Now that I was a front man, all those things led to a case of LSD—lead singer disease.

Even with this disease, I was completely devoted to my band-mates. I fought for them. I lived for them. When I got attention for writing the lyrics to our songs, I tried to turn the focus to Mark, Brian, and Flip. I'd say, "None of this could have happened without them." I spoke the truth. Creed was a band. Not backup instruments for Scott Stapp, but a truly organic musical unit.

Because my bandmates were reluctant speakers and I was not, I was thrust into the role of spokesperson. They didn't object. I think they even felt relieved that someone was willing to answer the media's unrelenting questions.

Like many bandmates who suddenly discover they are finding favor with an ever-growing group of fans, we were in a honeymoon phase that lasted all of 1997 and well into 1998. Everything was starting to click. We had few arguments. We were a group of guys banded together by a dream, a family not about to let anyone or anything get in our way.

Over the next two years, *My Own Prison* scored four number one songs—the title song, "Torn," "What's This Life For," and "One." The buildup to the megasuccess of this album took months of grueling and grinding on tour. But once the singles started to hit and we moved into half arenas, it wasn't long before we filled full arenas. And when we returned to New York less than a year later, it wasn't to play the Lone Star Cafe but Madison Square Garden as the opening act for Van Halen.

That concert was our chance to prove that we belonged in the big leagues. We were determined to absolutely slay the Van Halen audience—and we did.

In the pantheon of classic rockers, Van Halen's status is undisputed. I have utmost respect for them, and I don't think it's taking anything away from them to say that, despite their iconic status, no fan left that concert in the summer of 1998 without remembering Creed.

After the show Eddie Van Halen walked into our dressing room.

"I've got four pieces of advice for you, if you wanna hear it," he said. We did.

"Number one, never pay a manager more than 20 percent. Number two, after you check into your hotel, write your room number on your key and put it in your wallet. That way when you pass out, they'll throw you in the right bed. Number three, sign every autograph. And number four, never let anything come between you guys."

With that, he walked out.

*   *   *

We went on to tour the world and found armies of fans in London, Paris, Amsterdam, Tokyo, and Sydney. It was hard to believe that this was happening to a ragtag college bar band from Tallahassee.

In Paris we made the pilgrimage to the cemetery where Jim Morrison is buried. He was the one who led me to Florida State, where our band was born. He was the one who showed me that poetry and rock could be forged into a single expression. This master of rock romanticism had died at age twenty-seven. I was twenty-five.

Like John Keats, he represented the death of beauty at a tragically young age. Both men had made an early exit yet had gifted the world with their exquisite art. Was it my fate to follow Morrison to an early death? Would the same bewildering stardom that had destroyed Morrison destroy me? Or was I flattering myself to even make the comparison? Was I ego-tripping to imagine that I would be remembered as someone even remotely as gifted as the leader of The Doors?

The Greek lettering on Morrison's tombstone means, "True to his own spirit."

What did it mean to be true to mine?

In spite of my wanderings, I knew my spirit was in Christ. My job was to allow His Spirit to lead me through the dream world of rock and roll.

This world was becoming more than a dream, though. It was a reality that hardly seemed real.

At the same time, after shows and between shows, I began to feel drastic letdowns. To a certain extent that is normal, of course. Being onstage is a tremendous high, and postperformance letdowns are to be expected. But my lows took me deeper and deeper into a dark place.

I started looking for ways to cope. When I smoked pot on occasion, my fantasies intensified. At times my drinking led to blackouts—an obvious danger sign. Had I been sober on a continual basis, I might have recognized the signs that had been there since I was a child: I was struggling with serious depression.

My mother had seen this tendency since I was in elementary school. There had been talk about medication, but she had felt the risks were too great at my young age. As for Steve Stapp, I'm not sure he had the sensitivity to even see that I had depression issues. Even if he did, he had no faith in psychopharmacological solutions to depression. Whatever was wrong, he thought he could beat it out of me.

As Creed took off, I started self-medicating more and more. Weed and alcohol served as my antidepressants.

So did getting onstage night after night, singing in front of thousands of people. My fans were an addiction of another kind.

The phenomenon of groupies became a factor in Creed's burgeoning career. How could it not? We were young, single rock stars who had hit the big time. Only Flip, who was with his high school sweetheart and future wife, didn't get sucked in. We wanted to be wanted. And while we may not have taken it to the extreme other bands did, we also didn't turn away the attention.

Eventually I decided that the best way to avoid the temptations was to settle down with one woman. Her name was Hillaree. There was youthful infatuation between us. Motivated by a very young love, we married.

* * *

No sane person would agree to go on a rock-and-roll tour for more than a few months. A yearlong tour is crazy. A two-year tour is even more insane. We toured for basically the first six years of Creed's existence. From my point of view, it began to feel like I was being slowly poisoned. I wanted to stop, but I couldn't.

"If you stop, your career is over," Alan Meltzer said. "You'll be quickly forgotten and you'll die. To survive in this business, you have to let us kill you. Then everyone wins and you'll be remembered forever."

In short, in order to survive in this business, I had to let Alan Meltzer kill me. It took me years to come to terms with such paradoxes. To this day, I'm not sure I have.

At the time, I had stars in my eyes, and I was willing to do whatever Alan told me to do. I was a hero destined to fulfill the hero's fate. I saw myself as someone who would not only elevate myself to the top but also carry everyone else in the band along with me. I had Christ in my life, but I had not learned the most obvious yet most difficult lesson Christ teaches—humility.

As God incarnate, Jesus possessed the humility to declare, over and over, that His mission was to do not His own will but His Father's. He did not enter the human fray as a bejeweled king or decorated warrior. He received neither accolades nor worldly rewards. He was homeless. He ministered to prostitutes and lepers. He was the object of scorn, not adulation. He was the opposite of a rock star. We were nothing alike.

In my midtwenties I was a young man steeped in the teachings of Jesus while deeply disillusioned by many who claimed to lead Jesus' church. In the silence of nighttime, I often cried out to God to teach me, comfort me, and lead me. I wanted to serve Him. But I also wanted to do what I wanted to do. I wanted it all. I didn't see how I could reconcile these two passions—a passion for God and a passion to satisfy my desires—so I didn't. A third passion prevailed—the passion to write songs that expressed my soul.

In my songs the contradictions did not have to be resolved. Paradoxes could remain paradoxes. I could ask questions and not have answers. I could reveal my struggles. I could write about my prayers. The music only required that I be true to what I was feeling. And I was feeling God in the music, no matter how severe my sin. The music kept me in constant conversation with God. For all my doubts and struggles, it was an honest conversation, and it still is.

As it turned out, my struggles were not atypical. Millions of other young men and women, many of whom were raised in religious homes, faced similar difficulties. They were seeking to reconcile the God they had been taught about by religious bigots or closed-minded preachers with the genuine love of God. As I conveyed my own search, not in a sermon or a book or a poem, but in a rock-and-roll song, it resonated powerfully with people. After all, rock and roll was the currency of my generation. Rock and roll didn't preach; it exploded. Rock and roll wasn't logical; it was emotional. Rock and roll was the language spoken by an army of fans haunted by the imagery of a God who was much bigger than they'd been led to believe.

My goal was never to make a clear statement about my religious beliefs through my music. It was enough to describe my struggle and hope that the message came through.

When it did, I was gratified. It was thrilling to be accepted, to have people connect with my music. Yet I had no earthly idea of the consequences of that acceptance. The righteous move would have been to give the glory to God. I now believe that's the only way we can ever escape the trappings of ego.

A wise man once said that ego acts like your best friend but really wants to kill you. But at the time I had no way of knowing what was coming. So rather than embrace my acceptance as a gift from God, I rolled it up and smoked it like a joint. I got high off that acceptance. After all, I was doing what virtually all rock stars have done. I was bathing in my glory.

You work hard, you put up with rejection, you live with frustration, and when you finally reach the top, you want to take a couple of victory laps. You want to strut. That's only natural. But what happens when you confuse yourself—your talents, your charisma, your creativity—with God?

Maybe it's the same thing that happens when you win the lottery. You no longer feel vulnerable. Your needs are met. You think you no longer need God because you not only possess the world's riches but also the world's love. You're fooled into thinking that's enough. For a while anyway.

In 1998, as our first album reached unprecedented international success—with six million records sold and still selling—we went back into the studio to record our second album, which would bring us even greater fortune and fame.

I felt invincible.

CHAPTER 15

A MAN OF CLAY

Just as I believe God is real, I think the devil exists as a literal power in the universe. I don't see God as a white-bearded old man in the sky, nor do I see the devil as a cartoon character in a red cape carrying a pitchfork. But I'm convinced these opposing energies—good and evil, light and dark, hope and despair—are operative in the world.

There is a life force, and there is a death force. Ultimately God's power will prevail, but here on earth these two powers compete ferociously in our heads and our hearts. How do we deal with that struggle—how do we vanquish the darkness? Is it through willpower alone? Is it through keeping the evil away with fasting and praying? Or is it through understanding the power of evil and accepting it as a reality in life?

When Mark and I started writing the second Creed record, I didn't have a clue how to answer any of those questions. All I could do was describe the opposites warring within me.

I described my idea for the cover illustration to Dan Tremonti, who rendered it perfectly. A man of clay, molded by the experiences in his life, reaches up to God in prayer or agony, asking Him to finish shaping him. He finds himself at the crossroads in an epic battle between good and evil.

I asked myself a question point-blank: *Are you ready?* This question became the name of a song from *Human Clay*, in which I envisioned myself voicing a character:

Hey, Mr. Hero, walking a thin, fine line
Under the microscope of life

I had the presence of mind to realize that the hero's complex I had long indulged was doing me no good. I saw that "heroes come and heroes go." I saw that a hero's pressure to be perfect was something I could not live with. But was I ready to abandon that myth?

Under the light of scrutiny, I realized I was obviously the antihero. I knew the day of reckoning was coming, and I was asking if I was prepared.

But the pressure I felt wasn't merely internal. After the success of *Prison* and before the release of *Clay*, we collided with a phenomenon that would shake the very foundations Creed had been built on.

One day I was walking through the grocery store. At that point I wasn't famous enough to be recognized by the average music fan. When I passed by the magazine rack, a couple of guys in their late teens were looking over the latest issue of *Spin* magazine.

"What do you think of Creed?" the first guy asked.

"Pretty cool," the second said.

"Never thought I'd like a Christian rock band."

"Is that what they are?"

"As far as I can tell."

"That's not cool."

"Not cool at all."

I didn't think all that much about the exchange. I chalked it up to a couple of guys who didn't really know what they were talking about. But then the issue kept coming back.

"Have you heard all this talk about us being a Christian band?" Mark asked one day.

"I've heard a couple of comments," I answered.

"Where's that coming from?"

"I don't know," I said. "I have no idea, man. It's not true."

"Well, people keep talking. What are we going to do about it?"

"I'll tell the press. I'll tell them we're just a rock-and-roll band."

"Are you sure this Christian label didn't come from you?"

"Why would it come from me?" I asked.

"Well, you're the only true-blue Christian in the band. And you're the one who does all the talking."

"Hey, man, I'd be the last person to call us a Christian band, because I know we're not. There *are* such things as Christian rock bands. They go around proselytizing. They quote Scripture and try to get people to believe in Christ."

"Wouldn't it make you happy if everyone believed in Christ?"

"Sure," I said, "but I'm not putting that in the lyrics."

Mark went back to picking his guitar, and I was left feeling a little uneasy.

The issue didn't go away. The Christian label stuck, and in the minds of many, including the media, that made us uncool. I had to wonder why the classification was applied to us in the first place. Did the mere inclusion of religious imagery and prayer, even if placed in a larger context of a secular song, make a band Christian?

I considered the lyrics in *Prison* and studied the words I was writing for *Clay*. These songs were hardly altar calls. Rather than promoting my religious past, I was questioning it. I wasn't selling my Christianity; I was struggling with it. The Christians I knew—with Steve Stapp leading the pack—might have even seen these lyrics as heresy. By no stretch of the imagination were they anti-Christian, but at the same time they couldn't be considered Christian creeds. My firm conviction was that the fans who responded to the lyrics also shared my struggles.

This misunderstanding and mislabeling caused me discomfort. Mark, Flip, Brian, and I had started a band in the purely secular rock tradition. We came out of a time when rock and roll ruled the radio. We didn't want to be Stryper, a Christian band that openly sought converts.

The other disturbing fact was this: I didn't want to be seen as a poster-boy Christian because I knew I wasn't living a straight-up Christian life. I was drinking and smoking weed. I was taking advantage of the perks of success. I didn't want to be seen as a hypocrite, and I resented those who put me in that position.

It was during this time that I wrote the song "What If," where I vent about being categorized in unfair ways.

> Feel I've been beaten down
> By the words of men who have no grounds
> Can't sleep beneath the trees of wisdom
> When your ax has cut the roots that feed them
> Forked tongues in bitter mouths
> Can drive a man to bleed from inside out

It was a dry time for me, personally and spiritually. God seemed far away, and I felt misunderstood by the very people I was trying to reach out to. In "Say I," I described what had become the landscape of my soul:

> The dust has finally settled on the field of human clay
> Just enough light has shone through
> To tell the night from the day
> We are incomplete and hollow
> For our maker has gone away

I was still challenging the core beliefs that had been drummed into me. In "Wrong Way," I said it directly. I might as well have been speaking face-to-face with Steve Stapp when I sang these words:

Somebody told me the wrong way

I wasn't looking to preach to other people, and I didn't want them to view me as someone who was trying to convert them. I just wanted to explore what it might look like to live another way:

I hope it was an answer so you might live
I hope I helped you live

Those times when I was able to get off the grid were few and far between. On those rare occasions I would get out in nature and try to leave behind the chaos I was experiencing, both on the outside and within my soul.

One day I was able to go back in my mind and reconnect to that time I'd stood in the waterfall in the Appalachian Mountains. I described that experience in "Faceless Man":

I spent a day by the river
It was quiet and the wind stood still . . .
It's funny how silence speaks sometimes when you're alone

I was seeking Christ, whose "yoke is easy" and whose "burden is light." But He is also the Christ who provides a moral compass:

He looked me right in the eyes
Direct and concise to remind me
To always do what's right

                        *   *   *

I'm certain the acceptance of *My Own Prison* made the writing process for *Clay* easier for both Mark and me. Our credentials as composers had been validated, and we were far more relaxed. The ideas flowed, and the songs seemed to write themselves. We did virtually no second-guessing. In terms of artistic goals, we were aiming even higher than we had on *Prison*.

"Higher," one of the album's three monster hits, imagines not the high of drugs but the high of heaven:

> *To a place where blind men see . . .*
> *To a place with golden streets*

I envisioned an escape from the complexities and contradictions of life on earth. I felt myself driven by a hunger to leave this world of hatred for a world of pure love. I wasn't trying to prescribe how we can get there; I had no rule book with entry requirements. All I knew was that I wanted to go higher into that realm where understanding replaces condemnation and empathy stands in for scorn. That was my sense of heaven.

In a way, the most spiritual of all the songs on that album was "With Arms Wide Open." It was about the most miraculous of all human phenomena: the birth of a child.

Hillaree called me while we were on the road to say that she was pregnant. Whatever else was happening in my life, this event had the most significant impact of all. Out of the news about my child was born the single most successful song Mark and I had ever written. We composed it in just a few minutes. The words came spilling out of me:

> *Well, I just heard the news today*
> *Seems my life is gonna change*

I close my eyes, begin to pray
Then tears of joy stream down my face

With arms wide open
Under the sunlight
Welcome to this place
I'll show you everything
With arms wide open

With arms wide open

Well, I don't know if I'm ready
To be the man I have to be
I'll take a breath, I'll take her by my side
We stand in awe, we've created life

Looking back at the moment of composition—the moment I discovered I'd be having my first child—I didn't think my self-esteem was especially low. But when I later heard myself sing the lyrics, I realized otherwise:

If I had just one wish
Only one demand
I hope he's not like me

My own internal divisions, mistakes, challenges, pain—anything negative about me—were enough to cause me to pray that they wouldn't be passed on to my son. I was determined to break the generational curse. I wanted to stop the spiritual bullying in a system that pitted a hellfire-and-brimstone God against His archnemesis, Satan. I wanted to demonstrate love to my son.

In seeking a loving name for our son, I found the right combination in Jagger Michael. Jagger means "one who carries a message," and Michael means "sent by God." Surely the message I'd received, at a time when Mark and I were still writing the songs for *Human Clay*, was simply that God was good.

Hillaree had a beautiful baby boy, born October 21, 1998. For the first time in my life, I had been introduced to pure, unconditional love. Nothing could have made me happier. In reading Proverbs and Psalms and the Gospels all over again, I started hearing God's voice from a different perspective. The Father was teaching me how to be a father.

*   *   *

When we went into the studio to record our second album, we had the experience and confidence of touring veterans. We all agreed that no one but John Kurzweg could be the producer. We couldn't imagine trusting our sound to anyone else.

From the outside, it looked like a picture-perfect time in my life. I was twenty-five years old, a young man with a high-profile career in rock and roll. I had proven myself as a singer and a writer. I could command the stage and harness the energy of thirty thousand screaming fans.

In Mark Tremonti, I had a writing partner who dazzled me with his musicality. He gave me the space to say what I needed to say. His guitar lines provoked my imagination and pushed me to even greater depths. And to top it off, we were turning out hits and making serious money.

In Scott Phillips and Brian Marshall, I had bandmates who understood, supported, and inspired me to be my best.

And at home, I now had a wife and a son—a family of my own.

Could it all be too good to be true? Was I living an illusion? Were fantasy and reality on a collision course?

Yes, yes, and yes.

On the surface my life had a shiny luster, but underneath there was enormous corrosion. As my runaway success was gathering momentum, so were the forces of my destruction. I didn't see them, but the signs were all around me. The tension was building, and a violent battle was about to be waged that would rage on for the next twelve years.

The one sign I couldn't ignore came on an otherwise carefree day on the golf course. It had to have been nothing other than the hand of God that stabbed me in the stomach. I felt pain like I'd never experienced before, and it brought me to my knees.

CHAPTER 16

TRAGEDY STRIKES

My anger's violent
But still I'm silent
When tragedy strikes at home

I WROTE THESE WORDS from "Wash Away Those Years," a song from *Human Clay*, not knowing how much they would apply to my own life.

Scott Phillips and I were golfing together, as we did every day we had a chance. It was a beautiful Tallahassee afternoon, and the winter sun was warm without being oppressive. The cloudless sky was a brilliant blue.

We were on the green at the ninth hole. I pulled my putter out of the golf bag, lined up my shot, and was about to swing when I felt an incredible pain in my stomach. I leaned over and started to moan.

Flip ran over to see what was wrong.

"I don't know," I said, "but I've got to get home."

As I drove to my house, I hunched over the wheel in pain. All I could think was, *I've got to get home, got to get home, got to get home.*

When I arrived and opened the door, Hillaree was out cold on the floor. Jagger, only a few months old, was next to her, hysterically crying and kicking his legs. I picked him up and tried to comfort him as I called 911.

Hillaree had tried to take her own life. Later I'd come to understand that she was suffering with extreme postpartum depression, but at the time it hit me as a shock.

After getting some help, Hillaree came home. But that marked the beginning of the end of our marriage. As hard as we tried to make it work, I lacked the understanding and compassion required to endure the situation. Ultimately, we split up. This was painful for both of us, but my main concern was my son. I desperately wanted to protect Jagger. Due to Hillaree's severe depression, I was given temporary custody. She never challenged that, and at age twenty-six, I became a single dad.

It was a privilege to raise a child alone, but it was also a challenge. For one thing, Jagger and I awoke at different times. As an infant, he was highly creative in his sleep patterns, and I was on a rock-and-roll schedule. I knew I couldn't do this without assistance.

I decided to move back to Orlando. This was the first time I'd been there since meeting with my biological father to get money for the motorcycle that took me to Tallahassee. Mark Tremonti had a house in a gated community in Orlando called Phillips Landing. I bought a home down the street from him. Being close to my best friend and writing partner was a comforting thought.

I was intent on being both a mother and a father to Jagger. I might have even gone overboard giving him what I thought a mother would. I looked online for breastfeeding simulators, but none of them seemed reliable. So I found myself in a rocking chair with my son in my arms, feeding him from a bottle round the clock. I knew I needed help.

That's one of the reasons I called my mother and sisters. I also wanted my son to have an extended family. My grandparents had been a tremendous source of strength for me, and I was hoping that the same might be true for Jagger. In spite of all the pain over the years, I decided that for my son's sake, it was worth the risk.

When I called my mother, she was happy to hear from me. The love between us had never diminished. She wanted to help and couldn't wait to meet Jagger. I went to their lavish new home on a day Dad was at his office. I still wasn't ready to see Steve Stapp.

"Oh, let me see the baby! My first grandson!" she exclaimed. "He looks just like you."

Mom and I picked up where we'd left off, as if nothing had happened.

"Mom," I said, "I want you to be a part of Jagger's life. I want him to have grandparents. But Dad has to understand that disciplining Jagger is my responsibility, not his. I don't want him laying a hand on Jagger—ever."

"Steve has changed," Mom promised. "He's been forced into a humility he's never known before."

"What happened?"

"His dental practice has slowed down. And this new home we had built cost so much. He might not admit this to you, but he has accumulated huge debt."

While Dad was having financial troubles, I suddenly had millions at my disposal. The idea of bailing out the man who said I'd never make it without him had a certain appeal. It spoke to my hero's complex—I could save my folks. In essence, I could buy back my family.

I did. I paid off the $800,000 mortgage on their house, as well as the rest of Dad's bills. All told, I gave my parents $1.5 million. And just like that, Steve cut his work days back to two and joined Creed's city league softball team.

"I want to thank you," Dad said after I'd saved him from near bankruptcy. "I feel like I have my son back. I also want to share something with you that I've never shared before. Before marrying your mother, I went through a nasty divorce that cost me a fortune. I had a drinking problem. Both those things destroyed my earning ability for a long time. But when I found Jesus, I found sobriety. And then I met your mother. I've wanted to put my financial house in order for a long time but could never manage it. With your help, I have. It's something I won't forget."

I'd never heard him speak this way. This was a new Steve Stapp. Or at least that's what I thought. Meanwhile, I felt that my prayer for forgiveness had been answered. I didn't want to continue to live with an angry heart. If I could put the past behind me and allow my parents back into my life, I was confident I'd have a better shot at stability.

*   *   *

Jagger went everywhere with me, even on the *Human Clay* tour. At every venue I had a room set up to look the same: a child's nursery/playroom. That was an unusual demand for a rock and roller, and some people accused me of being a diva, but I didn't care. In the midst of the craziness, I wanted Jagger to have some sense of normality.

Our second tour was even more successful than our first. *Clay* was outselling *Prison*, and Creed was exploding across the country. Ironically, though, Creed's meteoric rise—sparked by the release of *Human Clay*—marked the start of my long descent into psychopharmacological hell.

I was living in extremes at every level. As the crowds grew larger and the tour became longer and the sales got bigger, I became brasher. During my days off, when Jagger was back in Orlando with Mom, I was drinking more. After a show where we were received like idols, my ego went into overdrive.

The key to spiritual equanimity is to give God the glory, but I retained a lot of that glory for myself. I didn't want to be the person I was becoming—and yet part of me did. Who doesn't like being a rock star? Long before Creed got big, I'd made a vague pact with God that were I to attain fame, I would spread His Word. I would use rock and roll to espouse my beliefs.

But those beliefs were shot through with contradictions and doubts. I resisted the idea that we were a Christian band because I was increasingly viewing myself as a fallen Christian. I resented the label because it was causing my bandmates to resent me. I didn't want to represent Christianity knowing I was something less than a perfect Christian. My scrambled brain was telling me that being an imperfect Christian was worse than not being a Christian at all. I didn't want to be considered a hypocrite.

I couldn't stop the war inside my head. Sleep would never come. I'd toss and turn until five in the morning. When I'd finally drift off, it was only for an hour or two. I knew the next day was destined to be torture. The rigors of the road. A long bus ride. A cross-country plane trip. Rehearsal. Sound check. Press interviews. Meet and greets with contest-winning fans. And all of this followed by another sleepless night.

One morning when I awoke, my throat was so sore I could barely swallow.

"You sound a little raspy." It was Alan Meltzer, who showed up at one of our concerts.

"My throat's sore. I've been feeling sick for a week."

"Well, you need to see a doctor. You can't afford to mess with your throat."

"I don't have a doctor."

"I know the best doctors in the world. And don't worry about the cost. All you've got to do is take a few pictures with the doctor and his friends and sign a few autographs."

Alan got me a rock doctor.

"I'm giving you a shot of prednisone," the rock doc said.

"What is that?"

"It's a steroidal anti-inflammatory."

"Is it dangerous?"

"No. It's a miracle drug," he assured me. "An industry secret. From Ozzy to Cobain, it has worked wonders."

That special category of physician—the rock doctor—was new to me. I didn't understand that he had two main jobs: to keep the rock star happy and to make sure he keeps performing.

I was happy because my sore throat was gone, and Meltzer and the others were happy because I kept singing. What I didn't know, however, was that before long prednisone would start messing with my head and exacerbating my untreated depression.

I later learned that long-term use of prednisone, meaning more than seven months, can cause psychosis. The drug was also rapidly causing me to gain weight. As I started retaining water, I became bloated and began to look unhealthy and strange. When I felt down after the show, I'd self-medicate with a beer or a joint. A pattern had set in.

As naive as I was about rock doctors and their instant cures, I was also naive about where I should go, what I should do, and what I should say as Creed became more well known.

In Tampa we played a concert with Metallica. Another high-profile rocker was also in town. He and I had become friends a few months before, and he had jammed at my house. I liked him enormously—he was an easygoing, fun-loving musician who enjoyed writing and playing as much as I did.

That evening he invited me to his trailer, which was parked behind the venue. I dropped in after the show.

When I arrived, I saw that he was accompanied by a group of strippers. My first comment, in jest, was, "It's good to be king." I was repeating a line from Mel Brooks's *History of the World, Part I,* which I'd just seen with my bandmates. After drinking a beer, I left. I didn't think much of it.

When a tape emerged a few years later with me saying, "It's good to be king," it created a scandal. I don't know who edited the tape to make it look like I was part of an orgy—I never saw the tape—but by then it didn't matter. No one wanted to hear that I'd merely stopped by to say hello and just happened to walk into what amounted to a private strip club. Protesting only further solidified my image as a sinning Christian—which I was.

Meanwhile, the highs kept getting higher. Ten of our first eleven singles were number one hits. We toured the world in private jets, with former Navy SEALs serving as our full-time security. Hordes of fans followed us everywhere.

"You're a superstar," Diana Meltzer told me. She was at our Chicago concert, dressed in her typical all-black attire.

"We've been really blessed," I said.

"It's no freakin' blessing, Scott. It's your talent. I saw this. I was the first to see it in Tallahassee. Remember? I told everyone then, and I'm telling them now. Alan's here, that fat freak." She stopped to laugh. "But he's a genius at business. Anyway, stay healthy, Scott, and keep touring. You can't stop now. How you feeling, honey?"

"A little tired and run down."

"Didn't the doctors give you shots and meds for that?" Alan had just walked in the room.

"Yes, they gave me something for my sore throat. They said I had strep and an upper respiratory infection. The worst part, though, is I can't sleep."

"Well, just tell those doctors to give you something to help you sleep. You tell them I say it's all right. If you can't finish this thing, that would be a big problem."

"I hear you, Alan, and I won't let you down."

"You wouldn't just be letting me down. You'd be ruining every-one's career, and there would be two hundred stagehands out of work."

"I understand."

"You call anytime, night or day. Whatever you need, I'll get. You got my word on that. Pookie Poo, tell Scott about my word."

"Alan's a fat freak, but his word is better than a freakin' contract."

* * *

I pictured what was at stake. Eighteen semis rolling down the highway, filled with our massive staging and lighting equipment.

Twenty-two tour buses filled with band and crew.

Twenty thousand fans who had paid hard-earned money to hear us play. They would hate us if I didn't show.

In the beginning, I couldn't wait to tour. Even our funky van looked beautiful to me. Playing in front of ten people in a country-and-western bar didn't get me down. I knew we'd make it. No obstacle was too big.

And then we made it. Three to four months of the *Prison* tour turned into six months and then twelve months. Then Mark and I wrote *Clay*, and it broke big. Before we knew it, we were back on the road. I was glad, grateful even. *Clay* was proving that we could be one of the biggest bands in the world, and what could be sweeter? Any kid who had dreamed of rock-and-roll glory would do anything in his power to keep the glory coming.

The *Clay* tour went on and on—five months, ten months, then a year. We hit every venue, every major market. Why not Europe? And Asia? There was no region, no country, no major city we would ignore. *Keep on keeping on*—that was our mantra. The drive was there, and the drive would never die.

If rock and rollers don't possess crazy drive—in their music and their hearts—they simply can't compete. It's only the drive that keeps us working to achieve. Achieve what? *More.* More fans, more adulation, more money, more, more, more.

I like the way Joe Perry, the great Aerosmith guitarist, explains the phenomenon of a band taking off. "There's a point when it's bigger than you," he says. "It's out of control, but it's cool because you're going with it. First it's friends, then it's friends of friends, then the real word gets out, and suddenly there's something magic about the band and you hear that people are lining up for tickets, fighting for tickets, scalping tickets. Then you start playing places that are never big enough. . . . You aren't pushing it anymore. It's pushing you."

In other words, it's all good until, at some point, it all turns bad. For me, the bad manifested itself physically and spiritually. The prednisone was messing with my head, and even worse, it was keeping me from sleeping. After a show I'd stay up until four or five in the morning, tossing and turning. The next day I'd be worthless, my head a muddled mess.

It was back to the rock doc.

"I can't sleep," I said.

The doc wasn't concerned. "I've got just the thing for you."

"What is it?"

"Klonopin."

"It'll help?"

"You'll sleep like a baby," he assured me.

"Any side effects?"

"None to speak of."

"So I don't have to worry?"

"Just worry about putting on a great show," he said. "Let me worry about your medical needs."

Of course I knew what I really needed—and that was time off. But because the end of the tour was in sight—only a month to go and a mere twenty-four more gigs—that wasn't in the cards. Klonopin was. I took the stuff, and it knocked me out enough for me to sleep.

Within days I was hooked. I couldn't sleep without it. Only later would I learn that Klonopin is a benzodiazepine. It's used as an anti-seizure drug or to relieve panic attacks. In other words, it's strong medicine—far stronger than I'd imagined. And on top of all that, it was interacting with the significant doses of prednisone I was taking.

At the end of the *Clay* tour, I came stumbling home to Orlando and was literally carried into my home.

"You're a rock star," my friends said.

"You're a hero," my family said.

"You must be on top of the world," a local journalist said.

I wanted to say, "Actually, I feel like I'm going down fast."

But I didn't. There was work to do.

"We need to get another record out there," Alan Meltzer said.

"And right away," Diana echoed. "Your third record is going to be bigger than diamond. It'll be freakin' double diamond. You guys have had ten number one hits. No one has done that before so fast. Not even the Beatles. You're making history. How does it feel?"

"Great," I said. But in truth, it felt like I was dying.

I was acting like my parents at church—pretending I was something I wasn't.

I was supposed to fake it. Right?

CHAPTER 17

WEATHERED

"YOUR FATHER NEEDS more money," Mom told me.

"For what?" I couldn't believe what I was hearing.

"Our contractor made major mistakes on the house."

"I already paid off the house," I said. "Have Dad take out a line of credit."

"He already has. We're maxed out. We have to stabilize the foundation and buy a new roof."

"Why doesn't he ask me himself?"

"You know your father," Mom said. "He's a proud man."

"Too proud to ask for my money, but not too proud to take it."

"Your dad's a lot older now. He says he wishes he could have done things differently."

"I guess it took him having five children who want nothing to do with him to figure that out."

"Now, Scott. God wants you to forgive."

I didn't respond. There was an uncomfortable silence.

"You're the perfect son. You're the son every mother dreams of having."

Like always, she grabbed my cheeks, gave me a big kiss, and told me she loved me. I felt like a child again, embarrassed by her affection.

In the end, it was easier to give than not to give. It would be a long time before I learned you can't buy love.

Still, there was a part of me that liked my new situation. I did what I'd promised to do as a little boy: I returned home as a hero to heal all wounds. I was no longer a black sheep; instead, I was my family's savior.

But this victory was a dangerous one. I had nothing left to conquer. I had come full circle, yet I was still hurt and angry.

I was shocked by Dad's lack of respect and his inability to acknowledge that I had won. It was just like our last basketball game.

I was teaching Jagger about the God of love, yet that God was only in my head, not in my heart.

* * *

When it came to Creed, we were experiencing an eerie calm before the storm. Creed was about to go from four to three.

Brian Marshall was a lot like me. I think that's one of the reasons we became such good friends. Back in college, before the Creed explosion, we hung out all the time. We went fishing together and listened to Faith No More.

With his quirky humor, Brian had a unique way of making other people feel good. He laughed at everyone's jokes, even if he was the butt of them. After the band took off, Brian starting having a good time too often. We both had the same disease. It's just that alcohol and drugs took advantage of Brian before they got to me.

On our last three-week tour, Brian was so out of control the guys in the band employed our own style of intervention. We were concerned for his health, and we wanted to help him. We hired a companion/security man to be with him 24/7 and keep him on the right path. (Later we learned that the so-called sober security guy only added to the devil's cocktail by introducing Brian to the world of pills.)

When Brian missed sound check during the first week of the tour, we were concerned. We couldn't reach him or his sober security guy. When we finally got Brian on the phone, I said, "Dude, you missed sound check. Where are you?"

"Hey, Scotteeeeee, my brother. . . . We are rock stars. Do you feel like a rock star, baby? I do. Yeaaaaaaaaaaah!"

I couldn't help but laugh because this was the Brian I knew. But it was no time to joke around—this was serious business.

"Dude, Mark is ticked. Here he comes."

Mark took the phone. "Are you partying, Brian? We agreed before the tour that this wouldn't happen."

A few seconds passed. Mark's eyes went wide.

"What'd you say, Marshall? You're gonna do what? Are you kidding me? I'll destroy you!"

Mark handed me the phone. "I've had enough," he said. "It's him or me."

I went to see Brian the next day and told him Mark's position.

"Don't blame it on Mark," he said. "You've been plotting against me for months. You turned Mark against me."

"Dude, you need some sleep. You're getting really paranoid."

Brian leaned back in his recliner and looked at me. "Scott, I'm freaking out. Help me."

That same day the band met to discuss Brian's fate.

"There's nothing to discuss," Mark said. "It's him or me."

"Mark, I support you 100 percent," I said. "You know we're brothers. But Brian's our brother too, and he asked me for help. I assume he means rehab."

Mark sat there with his arms crossed. He said nothing.

"I'm ahead of you, Scott," our manager said. "I've already reached out to the Betty Ford Center."

No one said a word. We all left with the idea that we'd get together again when emotions weren't so high. I reassured Mark that, if push came to shove, I had his back. In my heart, I was still intent on helping Brian. But as it turned out, Brian wouldn't allow it.

That very night Brian got online and started bashing me. In that moment, I was sure the whole world was reading his tirades. That was the last straw. Not knowing what else to do, I ended our friendship.

Two days later Brian sued the rest of us in Creed in what became a long and messy legal ordeal. Finally it was settled: we bought back his shares, and Creed, once a quartet, was now a trio.

Even with Brian gone, I felt a rising tension with Mark. He blamed me for Creed's image as an uncool Christian band. The money and success were great, but Mark hated being seen as a member of a band of religious nerds. Yet all this was under the surface, as he was reluctant to express his sentiments to me.

Of all the emotions to deal with, I find passive aggression the toughest. It's difficult because the anger remains unspoken, unexpressed, and you can't offer a response. Then that anger is conveyed in subtle, hurtful, and insidious ways.

Our critics didn't help. They started labeling us as uncool. It wasn't long before the same was being said of our fans. How could you be cool if you followed an uncool band? Fortunately our fans didn't care about the judgment of the rock elite and the haters. They were touched by our music and continued to buy our records. They came to our concerts in the millions. Over the years we've had amazing fans, and I'll always be grateful for them.

Every rock band dreams of being on the cover of *Rolling Stone*. When *Prison* took off, we were sure it would happen then. It didn't. When *Clay* took off, we thought the same. Still, it didn't happen. It was only after a year of touring after *Clay* that the phone call came from our press agent.

"Scott," he said, "they want you on the cover of *Rolling Stone*."

"Great! Have you told Mark and Flip?"

"I'm still trying to figure out how to do that."

"What do you mean?"

"They just want you right now. They said they'd put the whole band on the cover later this year."

"Absolutely not. That can't happen."

"Well, what do you want me to do? Tell *Rolling Stone* no?"

"If it's not the whole band, I'm not doing the cover. I'm not losing my friends and my band over some magazine—I don't care how big the magazine is. Besides, I'm not a solo artist. I'm the lead singer for Creed."

"Maybe I can talk to Mark and Flip. I can show them how this will benefit the band."

"Do that, and they'll think I put you up to it. No, I'm not doing the cover without them."

"You're making a mistake, Scott."

"Look, tell *Rolling Stone* that I'll let the world know they're trying to break up my band. Because that's what would happen if I did the cover without them. End of discussion."

A week later the press agent called. "Well, sometimes you lose, and sometimes you win," he said. "This time we won."

"What are you talking about?"

"*Rolling Stone*. They're putting the band on the cover."

"All of us?"

"All of you."

I later learned that *Rolling Stone* was not happy. They interpreted my request as a demand from a spoiled, egotistical rocker. They spread that impression of me to the rock-and-roll press, and I was suddenly seen as a diva. It made no difference that I was only fighting for my band.

In February 2001 Mark and I went to LA, where we won a Grammy as composers for "With Arms Wide Open," named Best Rock Song.

On a night that should have been a celebration, I still felt an undercurrent of bitterness with Mark. Because the song was about my son, I was getting all the press attention. I tried to bring the focus back on Mark and our collaborative effort—after all, I couldn't have written the song without him—but somehow the story was about me as a rocker and a first-time dad.

*　*　*

Weathered was the perfect title for our third record: it was exactly how I was feeling at the time. The lyrics were the most autobiographical I had written to that point. I felt like I had no choice—I had to voice everything I was going through.

The storm of success had worn us out—or at least it had worn me out. I'd started withdrawing from prednisone and was having a tough time. It had become a monster chasing me into the dark corners of my mind. The only antidote that worked was the company of my son, Jagger, who had just turned three.

He was living with me in our house in Phillips Landing in Orlando, and every night we'd go into the backyard and watch the fireworks show from Disney World. In my son's eyes, I'd see the light of love. I'd witness his amazement and purity and wonder at a world where the sky could be lit with every color of the rainbow.

Night after night the show went on. Neither Jagger nor I ever got bored. It was like we were in some kind of fairy-tale world. Sometimes Jagger would sit in my lap; other times we'd stretch out on the lawn. He'd always hold my hand. He'd tell me how much he loved me and the fireworks.

"I love living here, Daddy."

"I love you, Jagger Michael, my little messenger sent from God.

Have you figured out your message yet? Have you figured out how you're going to change the world?"

I wanted our home to be a safe, secure environment for him. I wanted to find a woman who could be both a wife for me and a mother for him. The absence of his biological mother weighed on me. But at the time there was nothing I could do.

*　*　*

Mark and I wrote *Weathered* over a three-week period on the deck of my new yacht, which I kept in Daytona Beach. The emotions washed over me like an electrical storm. Despite all the underlying tension and unstated issues between us, we hung out like old friends, drinking beer, making each other laugh, and turning out deep songs. In an unexpected way, our friendship was being renewed.

In the title song, "Weathered," my subconscious came to the surface. A one-line prayer expressed my deepest feeling:

Simple living is my desperate cry

The complexities of the rock-and-roll lifestyle, the strained relationships with the other guys in the band, and the remnants of the chemicals running through me had me praying for a basic simplicity that seemed beyond my grasp.

I try to hold on but I'm calloused to the bone . . .
Maybe that's why I feel so alone

I had fallen into despair and didn't have the strength to hide my true emotions.

'Cause me, I'm rusted and weathered
Barely holdin' together

I'm covered with skin that peels
And it just won't heal

In the end, though, I had not given up. I wanted to "take all this pride / And leave it behind." It was either the believing Christian in me or the athlete who sang:

I choose to win
I choose to fight
To fight

Outside of myself, I didn't know whom I was fighting. I clearly felt that I was under attack, that I was dodging bullets. The song called "Bullets" says as much:

I'm trying to find a reason to live . . .
In my lifetime when I'm disgraced
By jealousy and lies
I laugh aloud 'cause my life
Has gotten inside someone else's mind

VH1 had done a *Behind the Music* on Creed in which I was the main focus. The producers had good intentions, but in the end it was a botched attempt to string together the elements in my life into a coherent narrative. The band thought it was going to be about Creed, but in the end, once again, it was about me.

The way the story was portrayed did not resemble my reality. Because it was one of the most watched of the *Behind the Music* shows, it added to what was becoming the public perception that Creed was a Christian band and I their rebellious leader.

Could I have explained myself if I had wanted to? And if I were to do so, what could I have said?

The truth is that only a book would have given justice to the range of emotions I was feeling. But I had neither the clarity nor the time to write something so comprehensive. I was busy writing the *Weathered* album with Mark, trying to keep our careers from falling out of the stratosphere of megasuccess.

The only way I could communicate my emotions was in the form of lyrics shot through with ambivalence and ambiguity. If I could have simplified the emotions to simple phrases, the list might have looked something like this:

I was afraid that I was becoming dependent on prescription drugs.

I was fearful that I was slipping into major depression.

I was resentful that my bandmates begrudged the unsolicited attention I got from the press.

I felt betrayed knowing my bandmates didn't support me and instead blamed me for the band's uncool Christian image.

I was hurt that my bandmates didn't say they appreciated my role in our success.

I was furious with my father—and myself—for the way my money had further eroded our relationship.

I was angry with segments of the Christian community for calling me a fake Christian, and I was equally angry with segments of the non-Christian community for calling me a wannabe Jesus.

I was determined to continue to write great songs and make great music.

I wanted Creed to stay on top and become rock legends in this battle we were waging for our true identity.

On *Weathered*, in a song called "Freedom Fighter," I wrote about my commitment to press on despite the opposition, to keep delivering the message that was burning inside me:

But our mission's set in stone
'Cause the writing's on the wall
I'll scream it from the mountain tops
Pride comes before a fall

Another song put this question on the line: "Who's Got My Back?" During this time when I felt let down by so many of the people who were supposed to have my back, the only way I knew to express myself was through my songs.

When all we have left is deceptive
So disconnected
So what is the truth now?

Weathered is, without a doubt, a record of desperation. You can hear that desperation in "One Last Breath":

It seems I found the road to nowhere
And I'm trying to escape
I yelled back when I heard thunder
But I'm down to one last breath . . .

I thought I found the road to somewhere
Somewhere in His grace
I cried out, heaven save me
But I'm down to one last breath

As I think back on that time when I wrote the songs for *Weathered*, I remember all the nights I spent in prayer, crying out for a connection that felt lost. My need for God was raw, and it showed. I'm learning that's a need that will never go away.

The sequence of songs on that album perfectly depicted my descent. I came out with blazing fire but gradually started running out of fuel. During this time I used to quote Def Leppard: "It's better to burn out than fade away." I had accepted my fate, and I knew it was coming.

Here's what I wrote in "My Sacrifice":

Hello, my friend
We meet again
It's been a while
Where should we begin? . . .

We've seen our share
Of ups and downs
Oh, how quickly life
Can turn around
In an instant

I could practically see the train wreck coming just ahead, but it felt like there was nothing I could do to stop it.

"Don't Stop Dancing" was written in an effort to inspire myself:

At times life is wicked and I just can't see the light
A silver lining sometimes isn't enough
To make some wrongs seem right

I was still caught up in despair.

At times life's unfair and you know it's plain to see
Hey, God, I know I'm just a dot in this world
Have You forgot about me?

The only thing that assuaged my fear of abandonment was a certain underlying tenacity:

But I know I must go on
Although I hurt I must be strong
Because inside I know that many feel this way

The exhortation in this song was meant for me as much as for other people, and I meant it with all my heart:

Don't stop dancing
Believe you can fly
Away, away

I expressed my final plea in "Lullaby," a song inspired by a classical piece written by Mark. The only thing I could say without ambivalence was, "Just give love to all."

Yet I had no idea how to love myself.

*   *   *

Weathered came out at the end of 2001 and debuted at number one, where it stayed for nearly six months.

Next up was the tour, billed as our biggest yet. The rehearsals were intense. I was conflicted about going back out on the road. Honestly, I would have preferred to stay home.

Jagger was in school, so he needed to stay in Orlando. I did the only thing I felt I could do—I entrusted him to my mother's care and prepared an eighteen-page instruction manual for Dad on how to raise my son without violence, hellfire, and brimstone. One of my sisters was there to make sure nothing went wrong. And yet I was uneasy.

All this time, I hadn't stopped drinking. Against my better judgment, I hadn't completely avoided bars. I'd also got into a few brawls.

"You're that dude with Creed, aren't you?" asked one patron who was clearly not a fan.

"I'm just one of the guys," I said.

"The guy who sings?"

I didn't deny it.

"I don't like the way you sing," he said.

I didn't respond. If I had, I would have said, "Who cares what you like?"

He wasn't about to leave it at that. He wanted to get a rise out of me.

"Who knows what the hell you're even singing about?"

I stayed silent.

"What the hell *are* you singing about?"

I shrugged my shoulders.

"Are you saying you're too stupid to understand your own songs?"

I nodded my head. "You got it, buddy. You understand."

"The only song I do understand is that 'With Arms Wide Open' one. That was your moneymaker, wasn't it? That's the one that took you to Mr. Big Time."

I started to walk away, but he followed me. "You're a sellout. You'd do anything to make a buck. How does it feel to exploit your own unborn baby?"

Even though he was making no sense, something snapped in me. The next thing I knew, I'd hit him with a combination left jab and right cross. He fell with a thump.

I could handle myself, I thought. I could handle my detractors. I could deck anyone who said anything that ticked me off. I had it together. . . .

Nothing could have been further from the truth. I was falling apart.

CHAPTER 18

TWO MP5 MACHINE GUNS

"Rusted and weathered / Barely holdin' together." The lyrics to "Weathered" were a blueprint of the extremes I was living in every area of my life. That song was a confession and also a plea for help. I was wiped out—physically and spiritually bankrupt.

I wanted the party, the glory, the money, the power, the fame. I wanted to be the hero. So I chose to go back to the rock doctor. If this cocktail of alcohol and drugs would relieve the pain and get me through this rough patch, I was willing to do anything. Even if it meant risking my life. Failure was not an option.

I blame no one but myself for creating this situation. No one put a gun to my head and forced the drugs down my throat. I chose the god of hedonistic redemption. It was about me. It was always about me. I was my problem, but I was everyone else's solution.

The Creed machine knew me well. The Creed machine played on my hero's complex. The Creed machine knew I wanted to save the day. People's words echoed in my ears: "We're counting on you. Don't let us down, no matter what."

Oh, the irony! The Creed machine demanded perfection, and perfection was something I knew well. I had been beaten by my father for my imperfection. And I was about to learn that show business gives beatings for imperfection too.

When the *Rolling Stone* cover story appeared in early 2002, Alan Meltzer was visiting my home.

"Great cover, Scott!" he said. "I've got some music and lyrics I think you and Mark can use on your next record. You know I wrote that rap part for Evanescence's 'Bring Me to Life.'"

I was beginning to see Alan for what he really was. My ego paled in comparison to his narcissism. As he spoke, I had an epiphany. I was no longer under my initial illusion that Alan was playing the role of a mobster on TV; the man *was* a mobster. This relationship wasn't that different from my relationship with Steve Stapp, a father who seemed to care for me and love me like a son only to become my competitor and nemesis.

"So have you read the article?" Alan asked.

"Not yet. I was waiting to hear if I should . . ."

Alan cut me off, reading the story out loud. When he got to the part about our critics, he raised his voice, quoting: "'Rarely has a band been more successful but received less critical respect.' You know, I can have my guys grab this writer and bury him in your backyard."

"Calm down, Alan." I laughed nervously. "Sometimes I don't know if you're joking. You're scaring me. Besides, who cares about critics? The music fans have spoken. That's all that matters."

"You're right. And now this *Weathered* tour is going to make history. Bigger than the Stones, bigger than Zep, bigger than the Beatles—that's what this tour is going to do." He barely took a breath before rattling off his plans. "We've already secured five stadiums. After reading this article, I'm thinking you guys should stay out there for twenty-four months, not eighteen. The whole world is waiting to see this tour. As long as you don't let everyone down, you will be a legend and the world will love you forever. *Rolling Stone* will have to pay for your story, and you'll get to write it yourself. Your entire life, from the day you were born, was to prepare for this *Weathered* tour. Don't choke."

"Come on, Alan. You know I'm the mailman. I deliver. But will we have scheduled breaks or time-outs? You know the band rule—no more than three and a half weeks on followed by three weeks off."

"Time off? Did you hear what I just said, Stapp? There ain't going to be stopping during this tour. No breaks. You don't need any. You're the iron man of rock and roll."

The iron man was covered with rust.

The iron man was made of clay.

The iron man was, as the song "Weathered" put it, "covered with skin that peels and it just won't heal."

The iron man was defeated before the fight.

The iron man had surrendered to avoid the battle.

The iron man was coming undone.

* * *

I wish there were a way to tell my story and avoid all the darkness. But there isn't, and I've grown tired of the tap dance. I've hidden the truth my entire life. The truth is that I suffered from depression. And woven into the tapestry of this despair was my willing participation in all the toxicity.

No matter how dark the clouds, the sun's radiant warmth can penetrate that darkness. But when those dark clouds stay for months at a time, the sun and even the memory of it go away. I felt as if my suffering would never stop. I began to doubt the sun would ever rise again. I'd made a mess of everything, and I believed the mess couldn't be repaired. I got to a point that it seemed like I ruined everything I touched.

Somehow I'd turned even my success into failure. I'd disgraced myself and the God I claimed to serve. I felt certain that He had forsaken me because I had forsaken Him. I had become a shell of myself—a grandiose, ego-inflated shadow of what I used to be. At some moments I was convinced there was only one escape that made sense. The only way out of this misery was to end it.

In the irreparable life, accept death, I thought. *Be a martyr. Go down in history with Hendrix, Bonham, Joplin, Morrison, and Cobain. Your death will make everyone happy. You're worth more dead than alive.*

I figured if I were gone, everyone would get what they wanted—an explosion in the press, a boost in business, endless sympathy. No one would resent me anymore for being the focus of attention. The guys would create a tribute band and replace me as singer. Their perceived headaches would be gone.

I was alone in my home being gang-tackled by these obsessive, deadly thoughts. My twisted reasoning pointed to one action and one action alone: self-annihilation. I wanted to exit my music career as I had entered—with an explosion.

With two fully automatic tactical assault rifles pointed at both sides of my battered brain, I was no longer shaking. My hands were as calm and steady as my father's. I took a long, deep breath and closed my eyes. It was time for goodbye.

I opened my eyes to take one last look at the land of the living—and there was a photograph of Jagger, staring straight at me. I loved his eyes. They spoke to me. The portrait on the wall had come to life.

"I love you, Daddy," I heard it say. "I need you, Daddy. Stop it, Daddy."

Bam! I fell to the floor, gasping for air, my entire body soaked in sweat, my eyes bulging out of my head. Trying to stand up, I stumbled and began sobbing uncontrollably.

I looked around the room at all the trophies of my so-called success. Screaming like Rambo, I unloaded thirty-six rounds of bullets on every award and achievement I had won with Creed. Glass was shattering. Bullet holes riddled the walls.

I had shot up my house. But I was alive.

Jagger's unconditional love had saved my life.

* * *

Just a few months after I hit bottom, it was time to go on the *Weathered* tour. I was still in a dark place, but I was operative.

Before the first date, we were due to make our second video for the album. The first, for "My Sacrifice," was directed by Dave Meyers and me. It was an apocalyptic Dalí-esque depiction of a drowning world. And I was drowning. I was on a mission to rescue myself. But it was only the purity I saw in the eyes of a child that would guide me into old age.

We called Dave for the next video, this one for "One Last Breath." Dave was good at what he did, and I knew he was in tune with my artistic vision. I was eager to get to the shoot early to hang out with Dave and meet the crew.

I was on I-4 heading west through downtown Orlando. Traffic forced me to come to a stop. A minute later a minivan going seventy miles per hour rammed into me from behind. I didn't go through the windshield, but I couldn't move my neck. I was suffering from severe whiplash, a herniated disc, and a major concussion. But instead of being rushed to the hospital to be checked out, I was picked up and rushed to the set of the video.

A rock doc was waiting for me when I arrived. He gave me a shot and a handful of pills. Someone handed me the phone. It was Alan Meltzer.

"We can't afford to cancel this shoot," he said. "Canceling will cost me a hundred thou. You're doing it."

"Sure, Alan, don't worry."

I sucked up the pain and went to makeup. In wardrobe, they put me in heavy leather pants. At the set I was instructed to get into a harness that lifted me twenty-five feet off the ground above a large, spinning fan to create the illusion that I was free-falling from the mountaintop. Meanwhile I was singing:

Please come now, I think I'm falling
I'm holding on to all I think is safe
It seems I found the road to nowhere
And I'm trying to escape

My back and neck were screaming with pain, my head was about to explode, and I was mentally out of it. The lyrics couldn't have been more appropriate:

I'm six feet from the edge and I'm thinking
That maybe six feet
Ain't so far down

Was this life imitating art or art imitating life? I tried not to think about it—philosophical questions were getting me nowhere.

After the shoot ended, I collapsed. The next day I told the band and management I had to postpone the tour. It was physically impossible for me to sing onstage. This time no amount of shots or pills could patch me up.

My bandmates reacted immediately:

"He staged the accident on purpose. He wanted to get out of the video shoot."

"He thinks he's better than us."

"He's trying to destroy Creed so he can start another band."

"It's always about him, never about us."

What's wrong with these people? I thought. *Do they really think I'd fake a car accident that nearly killed me? If they don't believe me, why don't we all meet with my doctors and go over the X-rays?*

I never answered the complaints. They were too outrageous to address. Besides, I needed all the energy I could muster to heal.

I had to escape the madness. So I hit mute. I took Jagger and went to Maui. There I was treated with island healing techniques that involved the mind, the body, the spirit, and the sea. I loved how island wisdom connected nature, humans, and God—just like my grandpa had done. Using this methodology, I accomplished in three months what would have taken me a year to achieve on the mainland. There was no medication.

Step by step, day by day, I was reclaiming my strength, my spirit.

* * *

I returned from Maui to start the 2002 *Weathered* tour. I was convinced that, given my remarkable healing, all would be well. But all was not well. I was about to embark upon the year from hell.

The *Weathered* shows were amazing, but behind the scenes the band was falling apart. Rumors, resentments, and petty jealousies were getting out of control. People who were concerned about their own interests were trying to divide us, playing to our already overblown egos. The stress of all the drama got to me.

After four months of touring, I started getting weaker. My worsening condition was becoming obvious. The cycle continued: Alan would call hysterically from New York; I would perform with a sore throat; the band would be convinced I was making it up; my sleep pattern would go haywire.

Soon I was back in the hands of rock docs and their quick-fix medications. Once a trim athlete who weighed a muscular 167 pounds, I was becoming a bloated caricature of myself. I ballooned to two hundred pounds. Night after night I was singing my guts out. I didn't want to let anyone down.

After two sold-out shows at the LA Forum, I made an appointment to see Dr. David Sugarman. His brother, Danny, had managed Jim Morrison and The Doors. My managers came along.

"Scott, I have to be honest," Dr. Sugarman said. "This is very serious."

"I assumed as much."

"After looking at your throat, I must tell you this: you have to stop the tour. You need a minimum of nine months of voice restriction. I see a callus. If you keep singing, that callus will become a node. The callus must be gone before you even think about singing again."

"I can't cancel this tour, Doc. Can't you give me a shot and refill these prescriptions?"

"Absolutely not. And I'll be contacting this 'doctor' to deal with him. He's killing you with these meds. Some of the combinations you're on are literally lethal."

I didn't respond. I couldn't argue with him.

"Listen, Scott, you've accomplished more than most artists have accomplished in their long careers. You're only in your late twenties. Now is the time to protect your health and take a break. Rest your instrument. If you don't do that, soon you won't have an instrument."

At that moment he asked my managers to leave the room. When we were alone, Dr. Sugarman said, "I saw firsthand what happened to Jim Morrison. I know the pressures. I know that for you it's a matter of life and death."

I agreed. I went back to my hotel to figure out how I was going to let my managers and band know that I had doctor's orders to stop the tour.

The next morning my manager arrived at my room. He said he had another doctor for me to see. I said that wasn't necessary. Dr. Sugarman had ordered me off the tour. My manager said that was exactly why we needed a second opinion.

The second opinion came from another rock doc. He had my shots and prescriptions ready. Rather than fight the power, I went along with it. Prednisone. Klonopin. Percocet.

I was a good patient and did what I was told. I returned to the hotel, hoping I'd made everyone happy. I hadn't.

The hostility among the band members was building. At one point Mark made it known that when we were onstage, he didn't want me singing in front of him. He wanted to be visible to the audience every minute of the show. He even moved his monitors to the front of the stage, forcing me to walk behind him.

Emotionally, he built a fence around himself. I was not welcome in his space. It was now clear that Mark wanted to be the front man—or at least he didn't want to share the stage with me. When I told him we needed to discuss what had become a ridiculous situation, he told me, "I have nothing to say."

The passive aggression was no longer so passive. Soon Scott Phillips—the same Scott who had once been my golf buddy seven days a week—was equally remote.

Some of this was completely understandable. My meds had me off balance. Even worse, I had started drinking all day, every day. I had given some subpar performances. It was clear to the fans and the press that I wasn't right. I was not myself.

An incident at the Allstate Arena in Chicago got international press coverage. I was at the point that I no longer trusted my bandmates. Then it came time to sing "Who's Got My Back?," which includes these words:

Who's got my back now?
When all we have left is deceptive
So disconnected
So what is the truth now?

I said to the audience, "Do you have my back?"
I heard a resounding "Yes!"
Turning to Mark and Flip, I said, "Well, I don't think these guys

have my back." And with that, I stretched out on the floor, my back flat on the ground, and sang the song in a supine position.

A few fans thought I had fallen down drunk. That wasn't the case, but I was definitely inebriated. I would have never done this had I been sober. Because of my intoxication, I made a point publicly that should have remained private. I performed the entire show, but I was far from my best.

After the show a couple of concertgoers claimed they'd had bad seats and wanted to be compensated in the form of free autographed merchandise. We gave them everything they asked for. The next thing we knew, they were on TV, talking about their lawsuit. They claimed I'd been so drunk I passed out onstage and didn't complete the show. Ultimately the suit was thrown out of court, but the incident became an urban legend.

There were also threats to my life—accusations that I was the Antichrist and should be crucified upside down. At one point we had to contact the FBI.

People close to me took out insurance policies on my life. *Why?* I wondered. *Are they expecting me to die? Do they know about my near suicide attempt? Is it obvious to everyone that I'm close to the end?*

I started having recurring nightmares that I was fat Elvis during his final days. No one is comparable to Elvis. But in some ways I felt like I was walking in his shoes. I even started calling myself Fat Elvis. It was a rock doc who gave Elvis all the meds that he—or his management—thought he needed.

I remembered how Elvis died—on the toilet. He was dealing with the side effects of some of the same meds I was on. My Elvis nightmares would end with me burning in the pits of hell—the same hell Steve Stapp and his God believed was the fate of all sinners.

One thing was clear: I was absolutely incapable of looking out for myself.

The end of this miserable tour felt like the end of my life.

After the tour, I was dropped off at my house in Phillips Landing, where I wasn't even in good enough shape to see Jagger. I was determined to get off the meds before that happened.

In the meantime, I suffered agonizing withdrawals. I was climbing the walls. I reached out to my bandmates for help, but they were off forming a new band with a new singer. They never checked up on me. They moved on, as if I had already died.

All I had left was Jagger and God. Somehow, in my desperate and broken state, I felt that God hadn't given up on me.

It was the grace of God, His love, that kept me alive. Despite the excruciating pain and mental anguish of being off the prescription drugs, despite feeling abandoned and betrayed, something inside me began planning a strategy for survival. I saw that survival meant getting off the grid.

Again my life was my own prison. I needed out.

CHAPTER 19

SWIMMING TO THE RAINBOW

I WAS SWIMMING in the Pacific off the coast of Maui. An afternoon thunderstorm had given way to a burst of sunshine. The warm water relaxed my body completely, and I felt like I could swim forever.

In the distance I saw a rainbow arching across the sky. It was a dream, a vision—a painting of soft pastels in pink, orange, and blue. I wanted to swim to the rainbow. I wanted to swim under it and through it. I wanted the soft colors of the rainbow to magically heal all the hurt that had been accumulating inside my heart. I wanted the rainbow to transform me.

Yet the rainbow eluded me. The faster I swam, the farther away it appeared. I knew it was there. I saw it with my eyes. Its reflection colored the ocean beneath. But no matter how intense my efforts, I couldn't catch it. Its close proximity was nothing more than an illusion. And if I viewed the rainbow as a symbol of my longed-for serenity, that, too, was an illusion.

Maui was beautiful, but the beauty was not to last.

*　*　*

Maui was part of my strategy for survival. The island had healed me once, and I was confident it could heal me again.

Shortly after going through my withdrawals, I took Jagger, who was five at the time, and moved to the Hawaiian Islands. It seemed the only sane move. I put Jagger in a good school. Every morning I'd drive him there, and every afternoon I'd pick him up. We lived on the beach, where every night we'd walk barefoot along the water's edge and watch the sun set. I'd cook Jagger dinner and tell him stories at bedtime. I spoke to him about how much I loved him. We held hands and prayed.

As for me, I spent a great deal of time in bed fighting off depression. I got hooked on cable news, and in the spring of 2003, I watched the Iraq War explode. If my energy was up, I played golf alone. I didn't drink or do drugs or date women. Practically no one around us had any idea I was a rock-and-roll singer, which was exactly how I wanted it.

Taking care of Jagger was enough. Taking care of my body was enough. Taking care of my mental and spiritual health was more than enough. Yet as much as I tried to discipline my mind to avoid thoughts of Creed, my thoughts were stubborn. From time to time I checked in with my bandmates.

I got Mark on the phone. "Hey, man," I said. "What's going on?"

"Not much."

"You guys okay?" I asked.

"Yeah, we're fine."

"What are you doing?"

"I can't talk now," Mark said. "I'm right in the middle of something. Gotta run."

It didn't take the most sensitive soul to see that our brotherhood, so long in the making, had been destroyed.

In an attempt to stay connected, I called Alan Meltzer.

"*Weathered* is up to seven million in sales and still climbing," he said. "Before it's over, your first three albums are going to sell thirty million units in the United States alone. MTV is still playing every video you ever made—and VH1 has them in heavy rotation. Pretty freakin' great, huh?"

"Hey, Alan," I said, "I just heard from my accounting guys at Moss Adams. During an audit, they discovered millions of unaccounted CDs from all over the world that we haven't been paid royalties on. But as soon as they brought this to your attention, you kicked the auditors out of your office and shut down the operation. How come?"

"Those guys you got are crooks. They just want to tie up your money. They'll make up all kinds of freakin' stuff just to stay on your payroll. I've never let you down, Scott. How could you doubt me? Look, I've got another call. Talk later. Best to your family."

Click.

I looked at the phone and realized there was nothing I could do. I had given other people all the control over my life—label chiefs, lawyers, managers, business managers. Isolated in Maui, I couldn't drive to their offices and check up on them.

For the next several days I called each of the people handling my affairs multiple times and never heard back. I felt abandoned. Later I found out that my fears had become reality: my handlers, including Alan Meltzer, had cut and run and were working with this new band Mark had formed.

My sister Amanda and my mom came to Maui to visit us. Within the first three hours, I felt like a loan officer at the bank. That broke my heart. I thought they wanted to see Jagger and me, when what they really wanted was money.

Still, for everything discouraging in my life, I had God. Maui brought me closer to Him. Maui is a place where it's impossible not to see, hear, and feel God everywhere you look.

I also looked at the psalms. They spoke to me like never before:

As the deer pants for streams of water,
    so my soul pants for you, my God.
My soul thirsts for God, for the living God.
    When can I go and meet with God?
My tears have been my food
    day and night,
while people say to me all day long,
    "Where is your God?"
These things I remember
    as I pour out my soul:
how I used to go to the house of God
    under the protection of the Mighty One
with shouts of joy and praise
    among the festive throng.

Why, my soul, are you downcast?
    Why so disturbed within me?
Put your hope in God,
    for I will yet praise him,
    my Savior and my God.

My soul is downcast within me;
    therefore I will remember you
from the land of the Jordan,
    the heights of Hermon—from Mount Mizar.
Deep calls to deep
    in the roar of your waterfalls;
all your waves and breakers
    have swept over me.

By day the LORD directs his love,
    at night his song is with me—
    a prayer to the God of my life.

I say to God my Rock,
    "Why have you forgotten me?
Why must I go about mourning,
    oppressed by the enemy?"
My bones suffer mortal agony
    as my foes taunt me,
saying to me all day long,
    "Where is your God?"

Why, my soul, are you downcast?
    Why so disturbed within me?
Put your hope in God,
    for I will yet praise him,
    my Savior and my God.

—PSALM 42

At a time when my soul was more downcast and disturbed than ever before, I desperately needed hope. I needed it for my son; I needed it for my musical future; I needed it for myself.

Vindicate me, my God,
    and plead my cause
    against an unfaithful nation.
Rescue me from those who are
    deceitful and wicked.
You are God my stronghold.
    Why have you rejected me?
Why must I go about mourning,
    oppressed by the enemy?

Send me your light and your faithful care,
 let them lead me;
let them bring me to your holy mountain,
 to the place where you dwell.
Then I will go to the altar of God,
 to God, my joy and my delight.
I will praise you with the lyre,
 O God, my God.

Why, my soul, are you downcast?
 Why so disturbed within me?
Put your hope in God,
 for I will yet praise him,
 my Savior and my God.

—PSALM 43

Reading these psalms reminded me that despite the twisted things I'd been taught about God as a child, there was one thing that still rang true: the Bible is the *living* Word of God. In that serene place, everything came together for me. God's words spoke to my heart as never before. God blessed me with new understanding.

As I read these passages, I fell to my knees and cried like a child. This was the Lord speaking to me, comforting me with His poetry.

*   *   *

As Jagger and I walked along the beach, as we prayed together when we woke up and before he went to bed, God was on our minds. We were in the palm of His hand. Jagger truly was my gift from God. To this day I thank God I was able to allow my young son to greet the world with arms wide open.

As Jagger grew older, our relationship became more beautiful. Even as a child, he was smart, quick-witted, and intuitive, if a bit argumentative. He was the most loving child a father could hope for. Even though I tried to shelter him from most of the chaos in my life, I suspect he knew when things were wrong with Daddy.

Every night when he slept, I put my hand on his cheek and prayed, "Father, I love You. Please protect my son." I put my hand over his heart. "Father, I love You," I prayed. "Please guide Jagger's heart with Yours." I put one hand over his face and another over his knees. "Father, I love You. Keep his body safe. Shelter him from all harm."

After a year in Maui, I had regained my strength. I needed to get back to the mainland, back to music. I had written pages of lyrics in Maui but no complete songs. I felt like I had a great deal to say. I felt alive. I needed to express what I was feeling. At the same time, I had no interest in making music with Creed.

Mark and Flip, who had reconnected with Brian Marshall, also had no interest in making music with me. They had continued with their new band and had found another lead singer. Even though I was moving on myself, this wounded me deeply. But I figured I had a choice: I could sit around and sulk, or I could use this as a spark to do something on my own. I decided I had sulked long enough.

According to the press reports, Creed's breakup was being blamed on me. I didn't know how to handle the situation, so I said nothing in response. I just wanted to make music. I now saw myself as a solo artist.

Jagger and I left paradise, and I'll forever remember its spectacular beauty and the healing it brought. Maui had been necessary. But now I felt the tide turning.

I saw my son and me returning to our home state. I saw myself getting back to work. I wanted to work in an ambience where jealousy and competition did not exist. I wanted to avoid the passive aggression that had broken the spiritual backbone of Creed. I wanted a new and fresh situation.

My son and I settled in Miami, where I bought a beautiful house on the bay. I wanted the quietude to continue, the calmness to expand. I wanted life to be gentle and good. I wanted God in the center of our life. I wanted to be left alone with my thoughts and my guitar and my son.

I wanted to embrace love and creativity. I wanted to avoid drama. I wanted to start over.

Was that too much to ask?

Would I be able to do it?

CHAPTER 20

THE GREAT DIVIDE

Welcome, friends
I have nothing to hide
The journey's end has left a mark inside
I'm sure you've heard the rumors, jealousies
And all the lies

THOSE ARE THE OPENING LINES of "Reach Out," the first song of my solo album, *The Great Divide*. There was no way to disguise my feelings. I was more driven than ever. I was pouring out my heart in my music. I was alone as I tried to purge the pain of the past.

At first I was a little apprehensive about being so vulnerable with my emotions, but gradually I started feeling free. This was where I wanted to be. In "Surround Me" I sang:

They say no man's an island
But I tend to disagree . . .

I'm lost inside my memory
I'm still in disbelief

This song was based on a prayer I'd written in Maui. I was pleading my case to God, begging Him for divine intervention. I was isolating myself from the world and asking Him to save me. I didn't want to run anymore. I wanted to remain still and let God heal my body, mind, and spirit.

I could have easily called the album *Broken*, another song that spelled out my condition:

Do you know what it feels like
To be broken and used, scared and confused
Yes, I know what it feels like

I was taught that we're all broken vessels. My life was living proof of that. But more than ever before, I felt condemned by my friends, my family, and the industry. I wanted to rise and serve my God, my music, and my son. I wanted to soar.

Inspired by a conversation I had with Jagger, I wrote, "You Will Soar." I was speaking my parting words to Jagger, reflecting on the time I'd been convinced I would die young:

If I had just one thing to say
Before my last breath fades away
Keep your head way up in the clouds

Having been close to death so many times, I was now exhilarated by life and looking to express my new love for God. I was looking for sublimity. In a song called "Sublime," I wrote:

If we just carry on
We will find a way

I never wanted to return to the darkness again. Not only did I have to face the great divide, I had to cross it.

I saw the great divide as a crossroads. My life came down to simple choices. One side was chaos, the other order. One side was misery, the other joy. Whatever divide existed in my personal relationships, I was committed to choosing love.

I saw "The Great Divide" as a fervent prayer. It was my attempt to reunite with the Holy Spirit, the *feeling* part of my relationship with God. I sang:

> *You have loved me when I was weak*
> *You have given unselfishly*
> *Kept me from falling, falling*
> *Everywhere but my knees*

I was grateful to have survived such a horrific period of addiction to prednisone, alcohol, painkillers, benzodiazepines, uppers, and downers; the psychosis of withdrawal; major depression; a frail, sick body; and the terror of living far from God.

As it says in Job 33, I felt that I had been robbed from the grave. I had poisoned myself for so long it was a miracle I had never overdosed. I knew only Jesus had kept me alive. And yet, standing six feet from the edge, I continued to return to the precipice more than once. The grave still called.

* * *

In my mind, success was no longer driving me. Art was. So was self-expression. *The Great Divide* was something I needed to get out there. And yet even after recording the album I needed so badly to complete, it was rough reentering the rock-and-roll world. I began to slip back into old habits. My rebirth had reignited my demons.

A new wave of depression hit with a vengeance. Since it came in the aftermath of writing songs for *The Great Divide*, perhaps it could have been called postpartum depression. These songs were my children. Once they were out of me, I found myself back in the devil's playground. I decided to play.

As my depression grew, *The Great Divide* recording sessions suffered tremendously. Maybe it was growing insecurity, maybe it was increasing fear, but I started self-medicating again. Rather than put up with my erratic behavior, my producer, John Kurzweg, left the project. I floundered.

I knew the songs were strong, but my mind-set was not right. With good cause, I wondered whether the Meltzers were behind the project. My success as a solo act decreased the chances of a Creed reunion. The Meltzers didn't hide their hunger for another Creed record. As a band, we had proven we could make the Meltzers millions. On my own, I hadn't proven a thing.

These were facts I didn't want to face. It was easier to pursue the flesh. I needed excitement to keep me going. I needed to fill a new void.

Most of all, I needed help. I went to a psychiatrist.

"What about your mother?" he asked.

"I love her dearly."

"And your father?"

"I have two."

"Tell me about them," he urged.

"They're both unavailable."

"What does that mean?"

"I can't talk to them."

"Why not?"

"One left me, and I left the other."

"Why?"

"I'm not sure why my first father left, but I'm sure I left my second father to escape abuse."

"Physical or emotional abuse?"

"All kinds."

"Have you tried to reconcile with either?"

"I have."

"And what happened?"

"Nothing."

"So you think your depression is rooted in your failed relationships with your fathers."

"I'm not saying that," I said. "You are. I came here to get your point of view. I already know my own."

"That you've been abandoned by one father and, in response, you abandoned the other?"

"I don't think I abandoned anyone," I said. "I've had to live my life my way."

"You mentioned your band. Do you feel like you've been abandoned by them?"

"Absolutely."

"And would there be any truth in their claim that you've abandoned them through your unpredictable behavior?"

"I could see how they might say that."

"So abandonment is the issue."

"If it is, how does that help me?"

"Understanding always helps," he said. "Insights illuminate."

"Illuminate what?"

"Your problems."

"I feel like I know my problems."

"Then why are you here?"

"I think I told you," I said. "I'm depressed. I want relief."

"You want antidepressants?"

"I've taken them. I've given you the list."

"I see." The psychiatrist looked over the menu of meds I'd taken. "The list is long." He stayed silent a long while. "Do you think these medicines have helped?"

I was getting frustrated. "I think I'm here because they haven't."

"So you're willing to try others?"

"Yes."

"Medicines," he said, "rather than talk therapy?"

"I'm here to talk. I'm willing to talk. Does it have to be one or the other?"

"No, I think it's both."

"I want to do both."

"Let's first deal with the meds. Then we'll talk about their effects."

"Fine."

It didn't turn out to be fine. The meds only exacerbated my condition. They increased my blackouts. When I went to talk therapy, I found myself incoherent and unresponsive. The therapist was frustrated with my inability to focus. I was frustrated with the therapist's inability to deal with my frustration.

I felt myself sinking. I was heading into the scariest period of my life, the darkest depression I'd faced yet. I was self-obsessed and paranoid, anxious and confused. It felt like my head was in a vise.

Talk therapy seemed like nothing but pop-psychology platitudes. I'd start analyzing the shrinks. In my wise-guy mode, I would tell them how their unresolved childhood issues were slanting their perception of my situation.

"Until you resolve those issues," I'd say, "you shouldn't be practicing psychology."

I didn't want them to see the headlines flashing inside my head— *You're a star! You're a fraud! You're a hero! You're a hypocrite! You deserve everything! You deserve nothing!*

Why couldn't I go to church? Why couldn't I turn to God? Why couldn't I get ahold of myself? The depression fueled the drink, and the drink fueled the depression. Despair set in and told me I would never get better. I hungered for restful sleep, but the second I slipped into unconsciousness, my dreams only made things worse.

I dreamed I was flying in a private jet with the band. The pilot suddenly died of a heart attack. I raced into the cockpit to take over the controls, only to crash into the side of a mountain.

I dreamed I was back in my childhood home in Orlando, where

my biological father and mother were nowhere to be found. I looked for them in the nearby woods, but the trees were on fire.

Fire burned through so many of my dreams. The fires of hell were always close by, lapping at my feet. The basketball court where I'd played as a boy was on fire. My prep school was on fire. The bars where Creed had played in Tallahassee burned to the ground. Fire consumed the Indian reservation where Grandpa had taken me as a boy.

In one dream I saw Jim Morrison running through a fire that was burning down the cemetery where he was buried in Paris. In the same cemetery, I came upon my own tombstone.

In my waking life, my new therapist asked about my dreams.

"Do you want to tell me about them?" he asked. "Do you want me to help you understand your dreams?"

"But what if I feel like I'm dreaming right now? What if I can't tell the difference between my waking life and my dream life?"

"Where does the fear come from?" he asked me.

"Reality. I know I'm killing myself, and I can't stop."

"Why can't you stop?"

"That's why I'm paying you. You tell me."

"Well, I'm trying to tell you to stop your destructive behavior. But I'm beginning to think you enjoy doing this to yourself."

I didn't say anything.

"You enjoy hurting everyone who loves you. You enjoy ruining your life."

"I wouldn't say that."

"I would. I would call it insanity. Doing the same thing over and over and expecting a different result is a form of insanity."

"Well, if you're telling me I'm insane, you're not the first person." With that, I got up. "We just had a breakthrough," I said. "Let's end on that note. Do you give refunds?"

I walked out. That night I went out drinking.

* * *

If only I could have started a conversation with God again, if only I could have gotten back to my music. But I had no song to sing. I didn't believe in anything, especially myself. After expressing my experiences of renewed faith in *The Great Divide*, the irony was this: the divide between discipline and art had widened dramatically.

I was so overwhelmed I didn't even consider going back and recutting the tracks. I lacked the clarity and commitment to supervise the production. My demo vocals were used because I never cut the finals. Although I had some of the best talent in the business working round the clock for five straight days, they couldn't finish anything without me present. The album was only half done.

As I watched TV one night, I saw a special describing a new procedure called rapid detox. I fixated on the program. Maybe this was what I'd been looking for. I was tired of endless talk therapy and pharmacological solutions to spiritual problems. I wanted a quick fix, and this looked painless. Even better, this treatment apparently required no effort. I'd be sleeping.

I flew across the country to Laguna Beach, where I was detoxed under anesthesia. Yet I still experienced withdrawals. I tried to take the edge off by checking in to the penthouse of a five-star resort. Eventually I began exercising, and within eight months, I was in the best shape of my adult life. But I was still running from God.

The only time I prayed was when I put Jagger to sleep. Part of our ritual was to pray blessings on the woman God had picked to be his mother and my wife. We'd pray that God would keep her safe and guide her to us. I felt selfish asking God for anything, so I'd have Jagger repeat my words. I felt confident God would hear Jagger, but at this point I didn't feel worthy of being heard.

I had lost sight of God's unfailing love.

CHAPTER 21

JACLYN

ONE OF THE THINGS I love about Dante's epic poem *Divine Comedy* is how the Roman poet Virgil, Dante's surrogate father, guides him through hell and purgatory. Yet it is a woman, Beatrice—"the blessed one"—who guides him through heaven.

Beatrice was the love of Dante's life. He met her as a youth, and even after her death at age twenty-four, he kept her in his heart for the rest of his life. In his poetic imagination, she was the one who led him to God. His ability to receive divine love was facilitated by the love of a woman.

That is my testimony as well. Were it not for Jaclyn Nesheiwat, I would be dead. She brought a light into my life that changed everything. The change did not happen instantly, and the darkness did not disappear altogether. My inner turmoil raged on. Even though Jaclyn pointed me to the purpose and hope God had for me, I slipped back into the abyss more than once. Yet the dynamic changed. I found an ally unlike any I'd had before. I discovered a kind of love and compassion I had never felt before.

It was December 31, 2004, New Year's Eve. I was home alone, feeling restless and bored. When some friends called and insisted that I meet them, I said yes. They were in a good mood. I wasn't. The monster of my depression was starting to rear its ugly head. When I arrived at the party, I couldn't feel the fun and get into the celebratory spirit.

"What's wrong, Scott?" a friend asked. "You look lost, brother."

"No, I'm okay. Rock on."

"It's New Year's Eve, man. It's all good. It's going to be a great 2005, isn't it?"

I said yes, but I was lying through my teeth. It's easy to lie to other people when you've gotten used to lying to yourself. I was the character I had created in "Justify," a song from *The Great Divide*. I was still dancing with the devil. So I said nothing and half smiled. In truth, I saw nothing good about 2005. All I saw was the continuation of a battle I was clearly losing.

As "Happy New Year" kisses and hugs went around, I stood apart. I wasn't looking at the fireworks outside; I was staring at the ground. More and more, I felt alone in the crowd. I could see people jumping up and down. I could see their mouths moving, but I couldn't hear a sound. Shortly after midnight, I got up to leave.

"Where you going, bro?"

"Home," I said.

"Man, the ball just dropped. The party has just begun."

"I've got to go. Happy New Year."

I snuck out with the sole intention of going home. As soon as I was out on the street, I looked over and saw a woman trying to hail a cab. She was stunning, but nothing like a South Beach girl. She was alone, minding her own business, completely composed. Her sophistication stood in stark contrast to the Miami party scene. She wore an elegant jacket and designer jeans. Her figure was shapely but conservatively adorned. She had lustrous brown hair and dark, radiant eyes that seemed to be smiling.

I had to meet her.

Fortunately, the traffic was fierce and no cabs were stopping.

"Hey, let me help you," I said. I felt like a little boy trying to impress a girl with his good manners. "I'm trying to get a cab too."

"That's okay," she said. "But thank you anyway."

I liked the sound of her voice—slightly raspy, sultry, and low.

I pulled a hundred-dollar bill out of my pocket and waved it in front of me as I screamed, "Cabbie! Cabbie!" A cab pulled over.

"Which way are you going?" I asked her.

"Down Lincoln Road."

"My place is on the way. I'll have him drop me off first."

She hesitated. She looked at me—not in my eyes, but *through* my eyes. A few seconds went by. In those seconds I felt that my life was on the line. Then, finally, she smiled. "Sure."

Once in the cab, we started chatting. I was glad she didn't know who I was. I was tired of thinking and talking about myself. I asked her questions, and as she spoke I felt hypnotized. During those minutes I forgot my troubles. She had a wonderful spirit about her—free and friendly and irresistibly sweet.

She introduced herself as Jaclyn Nesheiwat. As we talked, I found out she was working for a marketing firm in Orlando. I recognized the firm because my stepsister—one of Steve Stapp's children from his first marriage—had been employed there.

"Do you know Summer?" I asked.

"Oh, yes. She and I have worked together for six years. Are you the brother who plays with a band?"

"I am."

"Wow! This is one of those small-world things."

Jaclyn didn't realize that for me it was more than a small-world coincidence. I felt my life changing.

"Sorry I haven't heard of your band," she said. "But I might know some of the songs if I hear them."

We shared more small talk. She was kind to me and complimentary about my profession.

"How old are you, Jaclyn?" I asked.

"Twenty-three. How about you?"

"Thirty-one."

"You've got a great job. It's neat that you can pour out your soul and make people feel good. Must be incredible."

"Yes, it is."

She smiled as though she understood.

We continued to chat and learned we had a lot in common. She, too, had grown up in a little town outside Orlando. After she graduated college in Florida, she moved to New York City.

"I hope you don't have a husband and children there," I said.

"Oh, no," she laughed. "I'm Miss New York. It's a big responsibility."

"Miss New York, as in the beauty queen Miss New York?"

"Yes."

"Wow. I'm impressed."

"I love the job—traveling and especially working with young children. But it's nothing as adventurous as being a singer in a rock band."

"Your title gives me new respect for the people of New York. They've obviously made the right choice."

The cab pulled up to my house.

"This is where I get out," I said. "And this is the moment I have to ask you for your number. Can I call you when you get back to New York?"

"I'd love that," she said without a hint of coyness.

"Happy New Year, Jaclyn."

"Happy New Year, Scott."

A week later I called to see if she remembered me.

"I heard one of your records," she said.

"Which one?"

"*With Arms Wide Open*. It's so beautiful."

"It's about my son."

Silence. Then she said, "I didn't know you were married. I didn't know you had children."

"I'm not married, and Jagger is my only child. I've been a single dad since Jagger was an infant."

"Where's the mother?"

"I'm not certain. She had some problems. I haven't seen her or spoken to her since Jagger was a baby. Jagger doesn't remember her because he was too young."

We continued to talk long distance, exchanging thoughts and laughing together. I felt like a kid with butterflies. I was falling in love.

"You're fascinating to me," I said. "What's your background?"

"I'm Jordanian. Jordanian Christian."

"Do you have a big family?"

"Three sisters and a brother."

"Are your mom and dad still alive?"

"My dad passed away when we were young," she said. "Mom raised us single-handedly. I'm really close to her. She's an angel. And she's done an amazing job with all of us. My sister Julia became deputy assistant secretary of state in the Bureau of Energy Resources. My sister Dina is a lawyer who works for the top criminal defense attorney in the country. My sister Janette is a doctor. My brother, Danny, is going to law school. Mom not only became a registered nurse, she also headed the orthopedic clinic at Johns Hopkins Hospital. That's how I became involved in programs for abused children."

"Gosh, what was your mother's secret? I'd like to put it in a bottle and sell it. I'd love to meet her."

"I want to know about you, Scott. What kind of childhood did you have?"

"Complicated."

"You want to talk about it?"

"Do you have a couple of months to spare?"

"Sure. I think I can fit that in."

"I'd rather have that conversation with you face-to-face," I said. "When can that happen? Are you coming back to Florida anytime soon?"

"I wish I were, but I don't have any plans."

"Well, I actually called to tell you that I'm coming to New York," I said. "I'm part of the New York Giants Muscle Team fighting muscular dystrophy. There's a big charity event I'm attending."

"No way! I'm speaking at that same event!"

This was starting to feel like an answer to my prayer.

* * *

Before that New York trip, Jaclyn and I spoke every evening for hours on end, sometimes even falling asleep on the phone. I learned that her brother, Daniel, was also a single dad with full custody of his son, JonPaul, who was Jagger's exact age. How perfect! I imagined that Jagger and JonPaul would be like brothers.

With Jaclyn, there was no judgment or pretension, no moodiness or demands. She had a beautiful spirit. She calmed the inferno in my soul. Her heart was generous. She balanced my overserious mind with light, loving humor. She didn't know that the world I'd been struggling in for years even existed. Her perspective was refreshing. She was also the first woman I had ever met whom I could envision spending the rest of my life with.

I was falling madly in love.

We had a great time in New York. Her speech at the charity event was superb. I was beginning to think this woman was too good to be true.

I was ready to do anything I could to deepen our relationship.

"If you really want to date seriously," she said, "you'll have to meet my mother. She's very old-fashioned that way. Would you mind?"

"Let's go see her right away."

Hayat Nesheiwat was rightfully skeptical at first. She had raised five wonderful children on her own. They were all superachievers. Where did a rock and roller fit into this mix? Especially one with a checkered past?

Like her daughter, though, Mrs. Nesheiwat showed no prejudices. She didn't hold my profession against me—my long hair, my tattoos, my earrings. She saw me as a man who adored her daughter. And while I can't say that her daughter adored me yet, it was clear that Jaclyn was interested in seeing how this friendship might develop. And develop it did.

When Jaclyn came to Florida, the first thing I did was introduce her to Jagger. His reaction was the same as mine: love at first sight.

After she left, Jagger said, "Daddy, is this the mommy we prayed for?"

"I think so, Son," I said. "I believe she's the one."

*　*　*

At the end of the *Divine Comedy*, Dante finally encounters God's eternal light when he's led through heaven by Beatrice. Beatrice combines the earthly with the ethereal, the physical with the metaphysical, the flesh with the spirit. She gives Dante what he needs to complete his journey.

I had no doubt Jaclyn was doing the same for me. I knew she was my true love. With her guiding spirit, I could surely make it out of my own prison. Jaclyn had brought the light.

But underneath our divine love there were shadows of depression that I foolishly thought I could hide from her. I didn't want my unresolved issues to diminish our bliss. We were living a fairy-tale life, and I didn't want anything to ruin it. And yet ironically, in trying to keep my past from her, I almost did just that.

Jaclyn was not only the most sensitive woman I'd ever met but

201

also the most intelligent. She was fiercely loyal, extremely passionate, funny, and family focused. Unlike me, she was also incredibly organized. She gave order to my chaotic life. And to top it off, Jaclyn, a former tomboy and competitive athlete, loved watching sports and eating chicken wings as much as I did. It was like hanging out with one of my guy friends—except Jaclyn was smoking hot.

Her family was equally amazing. They were open and honest, and they loved and supported each other unconditionally. I fell in love with not only Jaclyn but also her mother, Hayat (whom the family calls Yuma), her uncle Sam, and all her brothers and sisters.

Ours was an old-fashioned courtship. We went to movies, where we held hands, ate popcorn, and shed tears over the love stories, knowing we were in the midst of an extraordinary love story of our own. We walked along the beach at sunset, strolled on starlit nights, and took romantic drives up and down the causeways of southern Florida, the sea on either side and the sun shining on my new and blessed life.

Jaclyn was—and is—a strong believer. She was the first true Christian woman I had fallen in love with. I never realized how important it was to have a soul mate who shared my core beliefs.

I formally proposed marriage, and she accepted. Suddenly I felt goodness all around me. Jagger felt it as well. Jaclyn embraced him as her son, and the bond between them remained loving, strong, and unbroken.

My marriage to Jaclyn on February 10, 2006, was a beautiful occasion. The only painful cloud over the day was that my parents chose not to attend. They didn't support my marriage because they realized Jaclyn saw through them and knew they were looking for what I could provide financially, not for a relationship built on love. They also saw that she had become Jagger's true mother. That meant they could no longer use my son to manipulate me for money.

Of course our honeymoon had to be on Maui, the island that represented healing and rebirth for me.

On our way there, we stopped at LAX to change planes. We had a couple of hours to kill. Seated in a VIP lounge, I bought everyone a round. This was typical behavior when I was drinking.

"I'm allergic to alcohol," said a hip-looking older guy seated next to me.

"Allergic?"

"Yeah, it's just like a food allergy—peanuts or shellfish."

"So what happens when you drink?"

"I break out in handcuffs."

"Wow," I said. "I've never heard it put like that before."

"Yeah, alcohol wants to arrest me and then take me to the firing squad."

"That's pretty dark, man. I just got married."

"Congratulations to you and your beautiful bride."

An hour and a few more drinks later, Jaclyn and I were walking to the gate. Up until this point, she had tolerated my behavior. After all, I was still in postwedding celebration mode. But now I was getting out of control. For the first time she saw the other side of me.

"You're scaring me," she said. "If you don't straighten up, they're not going to let you on the plane."

That's exactly what happened. The stewardess wouldn't let me board. She called security, claiming I was belligerent. The next thing I knew, I was being led away in handcuffs. They took me down to the station and held me for three hours.

We missed our flight and stayed in an airport hotel until I slept it off. When I woke up, I looked at my bride with shame and remorse. We went ahead on our honeymoon and, in spite of everything, had an amazing trip. But the blinders had fallen off Jaclyn's eyes.

*   *   *

A new cycle began. I'd stay sober for long months at a time, only to slip back into depression and start drinking again.

In one incident that made news, I came home drunk after being out all night. Jaclyn had been up all night worrying. When I turned up still intoxicated, Jaclyn didn't want me in the house. She was rightfully furious and hurt. She asked me to leave and sleep it off. I callously ignored her.

Jaclyn felt like she needed help, so she instinctively called the police. They presumed that there had been violence, even though that wasn't true. Jaclyn was the first to say that nothing along those lines had occurred. The police arrested me nonetheless. I was taken in, and they threw the book at me. Eventually the charges were dropped, but once the media got hold of the story, another untrue urban legend about me was born.

Looking back, I see that Jaclyn had every right to seek help in that situation. I was wrong to go off on that all-night binge. Still, I felt it was a shame the way the situation was handled and reported. Jaclyn and I were devastated, hurt, and embarrassed.

In spite of everything, these situations managed to bring Jaclyn and me even closer. Our challenges had an upside: they made our marriage stronger. We believed in the sanctity of family and marriage, and we were not about to throw in the towel.

In the summer of 2006 the news of Jaclyn's pregnancy brought us much joy. Jaclyn and I bought our first home on a small lake in Boca Raton. I had even greater motivation to walk the righteous path and avoid anything that took me away from my family.

One day everything seemed to be perfect, and then, seemingly overnight, nothing seemed right anymore. My depression returned, this time with a vengeance.

I found myself in a cloudy space. My perception of the world suddenly had no color, light, or music. It was like the bottom fell out. The hope and clarity I'd once had were gone. I began isolating myself from my family and the rest of the world. All I could focus on was how much was wrong in my life—and all I had lost. My suicidal fantasies reemerged. I thought it would be better for everyone if I were dead.

Another part of me—the reasonable part—was observing this fatal outlook, saying, *What's wrong with you? What about Jaclyn and Jagger and the baby on the way? You need help. You need to beg God for help.*

My way of resolving this internal conflict was to self-medicate. I couldn't do that at home. I didn't want my family to see me that way. So I headed to Miami.

I thought about the guy at the VIP lounge. I had what he described—an allergy. I called it my nemesis. Whatever you want to call it, it was calling me. The next thing I knew, I was in the penthouse suite of the Delano Hotel.

I stayed up for three nights numbing myself. I was obliterated. Guilt and paranoia had set in. I looked around the room and saw nothing but the Miami-white walls, white marble floors, closed white blinds. My institutionalized insides were coming to the surface. In my mind, my penthouse turned into a scene from *One Flew over the Cuckoo's Nest*. The imaginary cops were after me. I had to get out.

So I hung off the balcony and considered swinging down onto the balcony below. It didn't matter that I was sixteen stories up. I was an athlete. I could pull it off. I stood at the edge. I looked over. I put one leg over the rail and then, as if in a dream, I fell into the night. Time stood still. Everything was in slow motion. I could see the air moving past me and, in between, the sky decorated with stars.

Amid the beauty of this free fall, I could hear hideous laughing. The laughter grew louder and louder, as if thousands of demons were welcoming me to my death.

Then everything went to absolute black. I felt weightless, floating on air. There were no sounds. Suddenly I was wrapped in images of my life, playing in rewind from that moment until I was in my mother's womb. There I was perfectly safe, warm, fulfilled. I saw a glimmer of light. The glimmer flashed, and I could hear the waves crashing from the ocean. I could hear the city of Miami breathing.

I opened my eyes and saw that I was lying on cement. I could not move.

CHAPTER 22

CROSSING THE GREAT DIVIDE

In "Surrender," an unrecorded song I wrote with a friend, there's an apt depiction of my condition when I woke up in the hospital:

So true, there's nothing for love to do
A war is raging inside your head
How long until you're naked, beaten, and dead?
Surrender

I felt some sensations in my limbs, but when I opened my eyes, everything was blurry. Through my cloudy vision, I saw two angels on their knees washing my feet, which were covered with blood and dirt. I thought I was being prepared for heaven. As I began to focus, the angels looked up at me. Tears started streaming down my face when I realized the angels were Jaclyn and her mother. I *was* in heaven. I had been surrounded by angels all along.

Compassion and forgiveness were the hallmarks of Jaclyn and her family. Throughout my recovery, my wife and my mother-in-law never left my side. They were pillars of strength. Throughout this storm we prayed for the sun to rise.

It did less than two months later, on January 4, 2007, when our precious daughter, Milan Hayat Stapp, was born. Milan means "gracious" or "to have the mind of God." Her middle name, Hayat, is after her grandmother, and it means "giver of life." Few other people have given me more life than Jaclyn's mom.

From the beginning, Milan was Daddy's girl, my twin soul without the damage. She forever changed my life. She continues to teach me what her mother started—how to relearn love. God sent me another angel.

Another blessing came in the form of service—the Armed Forces Entertainment, to be exact. In 2008 a representative of the organization contacted me. He knew I had a history playing for the troops and had volunteered to help any way I could. When he asked if I was available to do a military tour, I jumped at the chance. After I passed the physical, I received classified orders from the Department of Defense.

When I was issued a helmet, boots, and a Kevlar vest to protect me from possible gunfire, I was caught off guard. I didn't fully understand what I had volunteered for. But things were moving so fast, I just went along with the program.

I was sent to undisclosed forward-located military positions in the Middle East. Recalling my childhood hero, I was thrilled when I found out one of the locations I was flying to was the USS *Ronald Reagan* in the middle of the Gulf of Oman. I also flew in a C-130 with Navy SEALs to Djibouti, Africa—just north of Somalia—during heavy operations.

The experience affected me profoundly. This was my opportunity to live a boy's fantasy and be a soldier. Most important, it was a privilege to bring goodwill and music to brave men and women in harm's way who needed a night off and a break from the stress of war.

Back home, inspired by my trip, I was in a good place. Then came an interesting call. It was my manager.

"Hey, Scott. You back home safe?"

"Yes," I said. "Just spending time with the family."

"I've gotten nothing but good feedback from the military. They really appreciated what you did."

"I'm just a musician. Those guys are the heroes."

"Talking about musicians, I got a call from the guy who's managing your old bandmates. He was feeling me out to see if you would want to do a Creed *Greatest Hits* tour with the original band."

"What did you tell him?"

"I said I'd run the concept by you and get back to him."

I was conflicted. On one hand, I loved Creed. I felt that our fans had been abandoned, and I wanted to make it up to them. On the other hand, I was still dealing with unresolved hurt and anger. I also knew that our fans deserved more than a greatest hits tour. They deserved a new album. I didn't want to throw Creed in the past and create a legacy band. Creed had to be relevant again.

Finally I decided that without a new album, I'd have to pass on the reunion tour. That wasn't my idea of a comeback. Word came back that the guys didn't want to do a new record with me. A month went by. It looked like a standoff. Then their manager called and said they'd changed their minds and were willing to make a new record. They wanted to meet with me.

It had been six and a half years since I had last seen my brothers in Creed. Six years and six months was a long time for me to think about what had happened between us.

Yet the idea of reuniting was exciting on two fronts—I knew we still had great rock and roll in us, and I wanted to move beyond the past. I wanted to heal old wounds. I couldn't deny that I'd missed them and the music we made together. Moreover, Jaclyn and her family had put me in a loving and forgiving place.

I loved the idea that Creed would rise again.

CHAPTER 23

FULL CIRCLE

I SAW THE REUNION PROJECT as coming full circle—returning in spirit to our origins as a hungry college band from Tallahassee. We had been through it all, and now we were coming back to reintroduce ourselves and reestablish our rock credentials. We wanted to go back out there blazing. Our fans had waited long enough.

"Overcome" was the first song on *Full Circle*, and in many ways it was the record's emotional core. There were so many things we had to overcome as a band—the infighting, the petty jealousies, the ego trips. I had my own personal obstacles to overcome too.

These were the first words I sang on the album:

Don't cry victim to me

I wrote those words for myself. I realized that in order to escape the trap of depression and clear my head, I could no longer see myself as the victim. Victimization and depression are, after all, first cousins.

Everything we are and used to be
Is buried and gone
Now it's my turn to speak
It's my turn to expose and
Release what's been killing me . . .
It's impossible, impossible
Say goodbye, with no sympathy

I was struggling to say goodbye to all the negativity.

"I'm entitled to overcome," I wrote. My message was simple—no matter how many times you fall, you have to get back up again. You never run out of chances. That's what God's grace means to me: through Jesus Christ we're all entitled to overcome.

The origins of "Bread of Shame," a key song on *Full Circle*, go back to 2003, when Mel Gibson invited me, along with other artists— including Lauryn Hill and T.I., the rapper who rescued me at the Delano—to a private screening of *The Passion of the Christ*. Gibson wanted us to write for an album titled *The Passion of the Christ: Songs*. Included on the CD was my song "Relearn Love," cowritten with the God-loving hip-hop producer/composer 7 Aurelius.

Seven was another angel who came into my life at just the right time. At our sessions together, I had started to write "Bread of Shame":

When the world casts me down and says I've changed
I'll survive on all the promises you made to me
Guess there's no one to blame
When all you're living on is bread of shame . . .
When the world says I've changed . . .
Just promise me fame, I'll survive on the bread of shame

There were times I'd been living on the bread of shame. I felt all of us in the band had. That bread is as toxic as the culture of rock and roll itself. Blinded by the entitlement that comes with hypersuccess, we all made bad choices. We all had regrets.

In "A Thousand Faces" I was describing the visages of those managers and bandmates who had loved me and, in some instances, betrayed me. For all my dedication to this reunion, my doubts didn't disappear overnight.

In the song I asked, "How is stepping back a move forward?" I thought I knew the answer—that old wounds would heal and stronger bonds would be forged. But I couldn't be sure. I sang of my uncertainties:

Dug my grave, trashed my name
Yet here I stand, so you won't fade away

"Full Circle," the title cut on the album, sums up the mixed feelings I was experiencing—grateful to be back with my band brothers, with "one foot stuck in heaven," and at the same time scared to put myself out there to get hurt again, with "one boot stuck in hell."

Got your freedom now, boy
Who do you serve?
Took for granted what you should have preserved
No time left, no time left to make amends
Keep burning bridges while you're buying your new friends
A day of reflection hits, you're a shell, skin and bones, counting costs
Is it worth your soul? . . .

It's funny how times can change, rearrange, and distance makes
The pain fade away
So important then, doesn't matter now
Both feet on the ground
Come full circle, we've come full circle

I got one foot stuck in heaven, yeah
One boot stuck in hell
I looked at God, He winked at me
I made this mess myself
Don't be surprised and don't deny
Hear every word I say
Close the door and don't look back or you will fade away

Near the end of the album is the song "Good Fight," which was my way of communicating my commitment to press on, to keep fighting for what's right, even through the uncertainty. I was talking to anyone who, like myself, was "stuck somewhere between / Who I am and who I hope to be."

Full Circle was an expression of this good fight. Creatively, Creed was together again. And I credit my bandmates for putting their hearts and souls into making music with the kind of energy Creed fans had come to expect.

*   *   *

The guys decided not to use John Kurzweg, who had produced all three previous Creed albums. I fought hard for John, but the band wanted to go in a new direction. I conceded. Nothing wrong with a fresh start. Ironically, they chose producer Howard Benson, who had been slated to do my second solo record. Instead of doing that album, I committed to putting out *Full Circle* with Creed.

In the summer of 2009 my family and I lived in Beverly Hills while I went to the Bensons' LA studio. The entire album was recorded, mixed, and mastered in less than a month. Being in Hollywood was an incredible experience. I was certain big things were about to happen.

The record debuted at number two, under Michael Jackson, whose tragic death in June had rightfully overshadowed the announcement of Creed's reunion plans. I was crushed by Michael's passing. Like millions of his other fans, I'll always cherish the spirit in his music.

I wish I could report that the goals of the Creed reunion were met, but they weren't. Record sales were disappointing for a simple reason—Wind-up didn't promote it. This was the period when Alan Meltzer was lost in a dark drug addiction. On top of that, in true gangster style, he'd moved into an ultraexpensive penthouse atop one of the largest casinos in Las Vegas. By that point he had emerged as a celebrity on the high-stakes professional poker TV circuit.

Fatally for us, he had decided to sell the company to a group of his executives. It was in the interest of those executives for *Full Circle* to underperform and ultimately vanish. If it were anywhere near as successful as the other Creed albums, the price of Wind-up would jump by tens of millions. Consequently the record was sabotaged. If Alan hadn't been strung out on drugs and gambling away our royalties, he might have made certain that the album was promoted. But he was battling demons of his own.

Even with record sales slumping, as live performers we were still a hot commodity. We hit the road in midsummer 2009. Creed fans welcomed us back—with arms wide open, you might say. There were two American legs to the tour and a contractual commitment to do several international markets, including Europe, Latin America, and Australia. After the second part of the US tour, I was pumped to take our music overseas. Then came more good news: our live DVD was premiering in Miami and would soon be shown at select movie theaters in major cities.

Fans had flown in from around the country to meet us at the premiere in South Florida. Limos were waiting at my house to take us to the theater. Everyone from the band was there except Mark. I called him to see what was wrong.

"Hey, bro," I said. "Where are you?"

"I'm not coming. I'm ticked at the video director."

"Okay, I'm not thrilled with everything either. But people are waiting. It's a celebration. It's our first DVD. And these fans have paid good money to see you."

"I'm skipping it. I'm not supporting that director."

"Okay, I'll cover for you. I've got your back."

Mark was missed, but the evening was a success. After our talk, I thought all issues were resolved. I couldn't have been more mistaken.

Only a few days later, I was shocked to hear Mark's announcement that his other band was releasing their third record and had set dates for a European tour. They'd be going in Creed's place. Suddenly our international tour was off.

I was devastated. The Creed fans were being given the shaft again, and once more there was nothing I could do about it. This was the second time I was being betrayed and abandoned by my brothers.

Aside from the personal blow, the financial consequences were also significant. By postponing my second solo record to work on *Full Circle*, I had given up considerable income. This cancellation would cost me millions.

I felt I'd been misled. The intentions for reuniting Creed hadn't been sincere. The real purpose, it seemed to me, was to use Creed to generate promotional attention for their other band. To be fair, I had let them down on the first leg of the tour. Months before Mark's surprise announcement about his other tour, I'd had a bad night in Nashville. I drank and missed a studio session. I apologized to the guys and pulled myself together quickly. That was my only blemish throughout the first part of the tour. I thought I had more than made up for it during the second leg.

My bandmates may well have been waiting for a moment like Nashville as an excuse to drop me. I could understand that. I knew my past misadventures had hurt them. To return the hurt, though, especially at a point when we were advertising our brotherhood to the world, seemed like especially poor timing.

In any event, I had no choice but to go home. In their minds, I had injured them. Now they had injured me.

Full circle indeed.

CHAPTER 24

STEP BY STEP

My RECOVERY WAS, is, and always will be ongoing. I can't speak for others, but for me it will never be a sudden and permanent transformation. It's something I'm always going to have to work on and stay committed to. It's a reprieve that comes daily, based on spiritual maintenance.

After the abandoned international Creed tour in 2010, I could feel a depression coming. Alan Meltzer and Wind-up put a freeze on all my income, saying that the ongoing sale of the company meant all contracts were on hold. They wouldn't pay me the advance for my second album as promised. They stopped all my royalties. Alan also cut off all communication with me. He and Diana were in the middle of a messy divorce, meaning money would be held up even longer.

Stuck in limbo, I was filled with frustration. First no *Full Circle* tour; now no second solo album. My family was in financial need. It was time to start selling things.

I needed a break from the pressure. I needed to release my pent-up feelings. After what I had been going through, I felt like I deserved it.

I was in New York with Jaclyn, our kids, and the entire Nesheiwat clan for a beautiful family reunion. After the long flight, I wanted to stretch my legs and take a walk. On the way out, I decided to stop at the hotel bar. I told myself I'd get one drink only. Five drinks later, I was running down the street through the middle of Manhattan. I didn't know where I was going or why, but like Forrest Gump, I just kept running.

Through my credit card charges, Jaclyn traced me to a bar, where I'd passed out. She sent her brother to get me and take me back to the hotel. When I woke up, I couldn't recall a thing. Jaclyn insisted that I go to the emergency room. It was there that a clerk, an older man, leaned over and said, "Doesn't look to me like you need to be in an emergency room. You need to go to Willingway. I went there thirty years ago, and it saved my life."

I don't why, but something told me and Jaclyn to listen to this man. When we researched Willingway later that night, we learned it was a facility with a fine reputation in the field of recovery.

One of the things that troubled Jaclyn was that, before this binge in New York, there had been no indication that my resolve was weakening. Everything seemed normal. The next thing she knew, I had passed out in a bar. I could no longer deny my problems. I needed to go somewhere to deal with them. I made plans to go to Willingway.

I stayed at Willingway Hospital in Statesboro, Georgia, just outside Savannah, for forty-four days. For the first time I was able to see the absolute necessity of sobriety. I also saw how I required certain tools to embrace, extend, and deepen that sobriety.

So many layers of pain had been inflicted on my heart by other people and by myself. So many self-induced scars. Years of emotional chaos and acting out had taken a tremendous toll. I needed to address that chaos from every vantage point—medical, psychological, spiritual. I had to face the fact that my way wasn't working.

Willingway's staff was skillful, loving, and wise. They helped me focus on my relationship with God and on prayer. At times I felt like Job, smitten with boils. Only for me, it was my soul that was covered with boils. My heart was incredibly heavy, yet the burden was slowly being lifted. I knew it was up to God to do the lifting. In order to let Him, I just had to get out of my own way.

Willingway was old-school Twelve Steps. I saw the compatibility between that methodology and the path to salvation described in the New Testament. I learned that the origins of the Twelve-Step paradigm, as developed by Bill Wilson and Bob Smith in the 1930s, sprang from Christianity. At its core, the program is rooted in a belief in God. And although the notion of God has been expanded to "the God of your understanding," rather than the specific Christian God, the love ethos of Jesus is, to my mind, the driving engine behind recovery. To me the message was clear: I needed Someone greater than myself, Someone rooted in love, compassion, forgiveness, and grace, to get me out of my compulsion.

At age thirty-seven, despite all I'd been through, I didn't find it easy to admit I suffered from the diseases of alcoholism and addiction. But the evidence was overwhelming. The professionals confirmed that I had the allergy. Yet taking that first step of admitting I was powerless to manage my life—well, that went against my instincts. I had been managing myself since I'd run away from home as a teenager. I didn't know what it meant to willingly surrender control.

Even though control was an illusion, it was an illusion I'd completely bought into. Time and time again, rather than admit that my life was unmanageable, I kept holding on, managing to hurt everyone I loved along the way. Now I saw that this disease was something I could no longer manage. It was managing me.

The second step was far easier. For many doubters it is a leap of faith to come to believe that "a Power greater than ourselves could restore us to sanity." I give credit to everyone in my past—my grandmother, my grandfather, my mother, and even Steve Stapp—for indoctrinating me in God. The amount of time I studied the Bible helped me enormously. And although the circumstances surrounding my upbringing were troublesome, the fact remains: God's Word will never come back void.

I had absorbed the stories of the Old Testament, the biblical characters, the Proverbs, the Psalms, Jesus' parables, Jesus' sermons, and Jesus' life lessons. I knew Scripture chapter, verse, and line, and although during most of my life I had ignored what I'd learned, when I got to a point of sufficient clarity, I was able to tap those resources. I could believe that God would restore me.

The program's third step is also gospel-based—to make a decision to "turn our will and our lives over to the care of God." That's exactly what Christ's life represented. His entire mission was to do His Father's will. He modeled in dramatic ways what it looks like to surrender to God.

For me, Willingway was all about learning the difference between willpower and willingness. Over and over throughout my life, my willpower had collapsed. Willingness, though, was about being willing to admit I couldn't do it alone. Willingness was an admission that I couldn't will myself to emotional and spiritual health. I had to lean on God to do that.

For me, the first three steps can be summarized in seven words:

1. Scott can't.
2. God can.
3. Scott lets God.

As I went through these steps, I was reapproaching the God I had learned to love as a child. That reapproach required a hard look at my ego. Without humbly surrendering to God, there could be no spiritual progress. And because I was a perfectionist, raised in an extreme environment that demanded perfection but expected failure, I had to accept another basic principle—that my recovery was a matter of progress, not perfection. No other approach could have worked. At the first sign of imperfection, I would have given up and said, "Since I'm not perfect, I might as well get back out there and go crazy." The attitude of *might as well* had undermined me countless times. *Might as well* was a kind of antimantra. It set me up rather than calmed me down.

As I went through the other steps, I started taking action. I did an enormous amount of work. I had to forgive others in order to forgive myself. And my way of healing relationships was not about words or promises; it was about how I lived life every day.

I went home to Jaclyn, Jagger, Milan, and our second son, Daniel Issam, born July 4, 2010. He was another incredible miracle in my life. Daniel means "God is my judge," and Issam means "God is my protector." Precious Daniel added enormous joy to our lives. Another new beginning.

Not for a minute did I presume that I was miraculously cured or even cured at all. I came to see "cured" as an erroneous concept. I had experienced too many previous binges to expect smooth sailing. And I was right.

*   *   *

I was plugged in. After my much-needed retreat at Willingway, I returned to my family a new man. I was through with letting depression control my life. I was through with using self-medication to run from my problems. I was through with disappointing and hurting everyone I loved. It was time to get back to work, to save the day, to make everyone proud of me again.

I wanted to immediately make up for every wrong I had ever

done. I wanted redemption. I wanted to earn my forgiveness from other people, but oddly enough, I had yet to forgive myself. I wanted everyone's confidence, and I viewed winning that confidence as a twenty-four-hour-a-day obligation. I figured if I worked hard enough, maybe my family and God would forgive me. I was doing penance, and there's no penance without pressure.

Six months after Willingway, the pressure was mounting. I had worked hard in every aspect of my life. I wanted an "attaboy" and a pat on the back for all my diligence. Didn't I know you're not supposed to be congratulated for doing the right thing? I'm not sure. All I knew was I thought I deserved a drink. One drink. One drink wouldn't hurt me. That wouldn't be self-medicating.

I fell back into my old ways of thinking: *I've worked out all the problems of the past. I'm new and improved. I can control myself. I'm in charge. Nothing bad will happen. This time it'll be different. I've matured.*

In the midst of these thoughts, my cell phone rang.

"Where are you, Scott?" Jaclyn asked. "You said you were coming home an hour ago."

"I've just stopped to get gas. I'll be home in a half hour."

"Okay, honey. I love you."

"Love you too."

I drove by a bar. I didn't want to stop. I did want to stop. I stopped.

Five hours later, I woke up alone in a hotel room. It was 6 a.m. I immediately called Jaclyn.

"Scott, are you okay? What happened? I've been frantic. I almost called the police to report you missing. You've worried me and the whole family."

"I'm so sorry. I just wanted to have one drink."

"You had a drink!"

The pain I heard in her voice was more than I could bear.

SCOTT STAPP

I had failed again. What was I thinking? Everything I'd done in the past six months was in vain. How had one drink turned into self-annihilation? After having been given all the answers, I blatantly ignored them. In the span of one evening, I threw it all away.

But God bless my wife. Any other woman would have thrown up her hands in despair and left. But Jaclyn is not any other woman. Later that morning, when I returned home, she was waiting for me at the door.

"I want you to go to the Betty Ford Center," she said. "It's the best in the world."

"Last night was just a minor blip, honey," I said. "Remember— this is about progress, not perfection. I'm going to a meeting."

"You need more than a meeting. This is serious. Your life is on the line. I need a husband, and our children need a father."

That last statement really got to me. I stopped arguing. Part of me thought Jaclyn was overreacting, while another part of me was scared to death. Either way, I was on a plane to California headed to the Betty Ford Center.

When I arrived, the staff stressed the need for a program that included my family. I called Jaclyn, and she agreed that she, our children, and Jaclyn's mother would spend the summer in Rancho Mirage, home of the BFC. We'd be in the desert together for twelve weeks. Jaclyn and her mother never failed to stand by my side.

We were blessed by the presence of an advocate named Jimmy Weiss, a staffer who worked hands-on with selected families. Jimmy was our personal Moses. He patiently and lovingly walked us through the experience. At times, with the lecture hall talks and assignments, it felt like college. Other times we were ushered into deep reflection and introspection through exercise, creative writing, and prayer. It was all about honest communication.

We met in peer groups and in one-on-one sessions. Everyone there was open, honest, and sincere. We all wanted to get and give

225

help. We met families from every walk of life—government officials, professional athletes, police officers, nurses, schoolteachers, airplane pilots, lawyers, firefighters, clergy, you name it. We realized that we were not alone.

The BFC afforded me my first opportunity to sit with family members and hear how my decisions had impacted each of them. Though much of that was hard for me to take in, I needed to hear it. The family dynamic approach was extremely powerful. I could no longer hide my feelings from my loved ones.

During my time at the BFC, I remembered a basketball game during my junior year of high school. I was called for a charge and loudly expressed my frustration to the referee. During the time-out, Steve Stapp marched down the bleachers, walked into our huddle, and pulled me out. "If you ever express any emotion like that again, positive or negative, I'll pull you out of the game," he told me. "I'll make you quit the team, and I'll wear your butt out."

When I told the story, someone at the BFC said, "Maybe that's why you pour all your emotions into your music."

At the BFC, no emotion was left unturned.

Over the course of the summer I received ongoing encouragement. I was especially surprised and inspired when Steven Tyler of Aerosmith called. He let me know that as lead singers we'd gone through a lot of the same stuff. For the sake of the band, we had nearly destroyed our voices. We'd let the adulation get to our heads and blow up our egos. We'd toyed with insanity and barely escaped with our lives. Steven couldn't have been more understanding.

"Hang in there, man," he said. "It doesn't look like it's gonna get better, but believe me, it will."

I needed to hear that from a veteran I so deeply admired. Steven still calls to check up on me.

With summer ending, it was time to get back to our lives and our future. I was ready to make music again.

Willingway had been one essential part of my recovery; Betty Ford was the second. The third is the rest of my life.

As soon as I got home, I found Twelve-Step meetings in Boca Raton. I needed to be with people who openly discussed their struggles. I needed to hear their hope. I needed this support structure.

The only way I could make it was by God's grace, one step at a time, one day at a time.

SINNER'S CREED

When I was at the BFC, I received a surprising phone call from Mark.

"Hey, Scott. How are you, man?"

"I'm good, Mark. Out here in the desert."

"Yeah, hope that works out for you."

"Have you seen Creed's Facebook page?" I asked. "It's up to almost two million followers."

"Wow."

"It seems like the Creed fans are ready for some music. How do you feel about that?"

"Hey, you know I love the fans," he said. "But just give me a little time. I don't want to make any decisions right now."

During that summer in the desert, I thought a lot about my Creed brothers. I had to. It was a source of conflict I had to resolve. Building a case about how they had injured me was hardly useful. We'd all beaten each other up badly enough already. And we all needed forgiveness. I couldn't deny the fact that Creed had grown bigger than any one person in the band. Creed meant something to its fans. We wanted to give back to them after they'd been so loyal to us.

It was in that spirit that Mark and I talked again. We knew what we needed to do: "Let's make some music."

And so Creed decided to reunite as a band. Fifteen years after our debut album, *My Own Prison*, came out, we were on the road again. It felt like a rebirth.

I'm thankful for reconciliations. I'm grateful when relationships are repaired. Still, I know that I'll never arrive—I'll always be a work in progress. And so will my relationships.

Alan Meltzer died in 2011 at the age of sixty-seven, and I mourned his passing. A year before his death, he had divorced Diana and completed the sale of Wind-up. There was massive inequity in terms of our royalties, and we've had to take legal action. Millions of dollars are at stake. It's my belief that the pending lawsuits will finally put the issue to rest. Alan was a brilliant, talented, and ruthless executive. Yet in spite of everything that transpired, he and Diana signed us when no one else would, and for that I will always be grateful.

As for my family, there are wounds from my stepfather, mother, and sisters that will never entirely go away. But when you serve a God of love, I believe forgiveness is possible. Not easy, but possible.

I want to heal my wounds and help heal the wounds of others. I want to live my life in peace. I pray for that peace to spread. I live every day to love God, my wife, and my beautiful children.

But in the end I know that I'm fatally flawed. In the end I'm a slave to one master. That master is sin.

After all is said and done, this is my Sinner's Creed:

I confess that I'm a sinner
Just like my old man

In word and in deed I enjoy my sin
In word and in deed my sin enjoys me
There is no one to blame
No one but me
Sin is my nature
I sin instinctually

Sin mimics the gates of paradise
Sin beats me to the floor
Sin is the dark shadow that no one can ignore
Sin screams, "What's yours I want"
Sin screams, "What's mine I'll keep"
Sin is forever knocking, beating at the iron door
Don't even open it for an instant
Sin always wants more

Sin forever stole the key
But you're not locked out forever
In this sinner's Garden of Eden
Where sin pretends to be a treasure
Sin wants to make you bleed

Sin cuts down every giver
Sin cuts every hand
Sin wants total control
Sin wants to command
Sin just wants to kill you
And, yes, for you the bell tolls

So death came before life entered
In death sin was conceived
Sin will linger forever
Blameless, it's part of you and me

But there's a silver lining to sin's story
And the silver lining is this—
When I was out chasing sin
The truth was out chasing me
And when it finally caught me
That truth set me free

Now I've shared it all
Perhaps I've shared too much
But in this you must believe
The only truth I have left
Is this, my Sinner's Creed

I've come to see sin as separation from God. In that respect, I've been a lifelong sinner, as evidenced by the countless times I've separated myself from Him. Those were acts of willfulness. I call this book *Sinner's Creed* because I realize that my life as a Christian has always been—and always will be—challenged by these periods of separation.

At the same time, sin is not the end of my story. I believe with all my heart that the living Christ, whom I love deeply, stays steady. He is there whenever we call Him. To praise His holy name is to do more than simply attend church. Sometimes it involves checking in to a hospital or going to a meeting or staying silent in the solitude of night. For me, it always means getting out of myself and into Him.

It feels good, after all these years, to say that I love Jesus and I love rock and roll. My passion for both is greater than ever before. I want to pursue my life as a Christian and grow my spirit, just as I want to grow my artistic expression.

I thank God for all that is good and great in this world. I thank Him for allowing me to tell my story. The glory is His.

SONG LYRICS

It's impossible for me to separate my life from my lyrics. They are as much a part of my story as the book you've just read. I include them here as another record—a poetic record—of the journey of my mind and my heart.

MY OWN PRISON
Creed Album #1, 1997

TORN

Peace is what they tell me
Love, am I unholy?
Lies are what they tell me
Despise you that control me

The peace is dead in my soul
I have blamed the reasons for
My intentions poor
Yes, I'm the one who
The only one who
Would carry on this far

Torn, I'm filthy
Born in my own misery
Stole all that you gave me
Control you claim you save me

The peace is dead in my soul
I have blamed the reasons for
My intentions poor
Yes, I'm the one who
The only one who
Would carry on this far

Peace in my head
Love in my head
Lies, lies, lies, lies in my head

The peace is dead in my soul
I have blamed the reasons for
My intentions poor
Yes, I'm the one who
The only one who
Would carry on this far

The peace is dead in my soul
I have blamed the reasons for
My intentions poor
Yes, I'm the one who
The only one who
Would carry on this far

ODE

Hang me, watch awhile
Let me see you smile as I die
Take me, as my body burns
Let me see you yearn, while I cry

One step on your own
And you walk all over me
One head in the clouds
You won't let go
You're too proud
One light to the blind, and they see
One touch on the head, we believe

Adore me as I drift away
Let me hear you say I'm fine
You cry as my body dies
All that you despised is gone away

One step on your own
And you walk all over me
One head in the clouds
You won't let go, you're too proud
One light to the blind, and they see
One touch on the head, we believe
We believe

One step on your own
And you walk all over me
One head in the clouds
You won't let go, you're too proud
One light to the blind, and they see
One touch on the head, we believe
We believe

MY OWN PRISON

A court is in session, a verdict is in
No appeal on the docket today
Just my own sin
The walls are cold and pale
The cage made of steel
Screams fill the room
Alone I drop and kneel

Silence now the sound
My breath the only motion around
Demons cluttering around
My face showing no emotion
Shackled by my sentence
Expecting no return
Here there is no penance
My skin begins to burn

(And I said, oh)
So I held my head up high
Hiding hate that burns inside
Which only fuels their selfish pride
(And I said, oh)
We're all held captive out from the sun
A sun that shines on only some
We the meek are all in one

I hear a thunder in the distance
See a vision of a cross
I feel the pain that was given
On that sad day of loss
A lion roars in the darkness
Only He holds the key
A light to free me from my burden
And grant me life eternally

Should've been dead
On a Sunday morning
Banging my head
No time for mourning
Ain't got no time

Should've been dead
On a Sunday morning
Banging my head
No time for mourning
Ain't got no time

(And I said, oh)

So I held my head up high
Hiding hate that burns inside
Which only fuels their selfish pride
(And I said, oh)
We're all held captive out from the sun
A sun that shines on only some
We the meek are all in one

I cry out to God
Seeking only His decision
Gabriel stands and confirms
I've created my own prison

I cry out to God
Seeking only His decision
Gabriel stands and confirms
I've created my own prison

(And I said, oh)
So I held my head up high
Hiding hate that burns inside
Which only fuels their selfish pride
We're all held captive out from the sun
A sun that shines on only some
We the meek are all in one

(And I said, oh)
So I held my head up high
Hiding hate that burns inside
Which only fuels their selfish pride
(And I said, oh)
We're all held captive out from the sun
A sun that shines on only some
We the meek are all in one

Should've been dead on a Sunday morning
Banging my head
No time for mourning
Ain't got no time

PITY FOR A DIME

An artificial season
Covered by summer rain
Losing all my reason
'Cause there's nothing left to blame
Shadows paint the sidewalk
A living picture in a frame
See the sea of people
All their faces look the same

So I sat down for awhile
Forcing a smile
In a state of self-denial
Is it worthwhile?
Sell my pity for a dime
Yeah, just one dime
Sell my pity for a dime
Yeah, just one dime

Plain talk can be the easy way
Signs of losing my faith
Losing my faith
Plain talk can be the easy way
Signs of losing my faith
Losing my faith

So I sat down for awhile
Yeah, forcing a smile
In a state of self-denial
Yeah, is it worthwhile?
Sell my pity for a dime
Yeah, just one dime
Sell my pity for a dime
Yeah, just one dime

So I sat down for awhile
Yeah, forcing a smile
In a state of self-denial
Yeah, is it worthwhile?
Sell my pity for a dime
Yeah, just one dime
Sell my pity for a dime
Yeah, just one dime

IN AMERICA

Only in America
We're slaves to be free
Only in America we kill the unborn
To make ends meet
Only in America
Sexuality is democracy
Only in America we stamp our dollar
"In God We Trust"

What is right or wrong?
I don't know who to believe in
My soul sings a different song
In America
What is right or wrong?
I don't know who to believe in
My soul sings a different song
In America, in America, in America

Church bell's ringing
Pass the plate around
The choir is singing
As their leader falls to the ground
Please, mister prophet man
Tell me which way to go
I gave my last dollar
Can I still come to your show?

[Chorus]

I am right and you are wrong
I am right and you are wrong
I am right and you are wrong
No one's right and no one's wrong
In America, in America, in America, in America

What is right or wrong?
I don't know who to believe in
My soul sings a different song
In America, in America

What is right or wrong?
I don't know who to believe in
My soul sings a different song
In America, in America
What is right for you and me?
In America

ILLUSION

The sun rises to another day
My constitution keeps changing
Till it slips away
So I lie awake and stare
My mind thinking, just wandering
Does anybody care?

Should I stay or go?
Should I sleep or stay awake?
Am I really happy or is it all
Just an illusion?

Sitting in my room now
Hiding thoughts
Just hoping one day I'll get out
I hear a voice call my name
Breaking trance, so silent
So I can stay the same

Should I stay or go?
Should I sleep or stay awake?
Am I really happy or is it all
Just an illusion?

Wait now, many things left unsaid
This life remains the same
But I change
I try to fool myself in believing
Things are going to get better
But life goes on

Should I stay or go?
Should I sleep or stay awake?
Am I really happy or is it all
Just an illusion?
Just an illusion
Just an illusion
Just an illusion
Just an illusion
Just an illusion
Just an illusion

UNFORGIVEN

I kept up with the prophecies you spoke
I kept up with the message inside
Lost sight of the irony of twisted faith
Lost sight of my soul and its void

Think I'm unforgiven to this world
Think I'm unforgiven to this world

Took a chance at deceiving myself
To share in the consequence of lies
Childish with my reasoning and pride
Godless to the extent that I died

Think I'm unforgiven to this world
Think I'm unforgiven to this world
Think I'm unforgiven

Step inside the light and see the fear
Of God burn inside of me
The gold was put to flame
To kill, to burn, to mold its purity

Think I'm unforgiven to this world
Think I'm unforgiven to this world
Think I'm unforgiven

SISTER

Caught up in the middle
Had no choice, had no choice
Birthright forgotten, so silent
No voice

I see you
You know who
Little sister, little sister
Now realize, little sister
Overlooked little girl
Now realize, little sister
Overlooked little girl

Bottled up and empty, holding back
At loss you're forgotten
Getting back, get back
Bottled up and empty, holding back
At loss you're forgotten
Getting back, get back
Get back, get back, yeah

Expectations of another
Love given to the younger
Broken father, broken brother
Emptiness feeds the hunger

I see you
You know who
Little sister, little sister

Now realize, little sister
Overlooked little girl
Now realize, little sister
Overlooked little girl

Bottled up and empty, holding back
At loss you're forgotten
Getting back, get back
Bottled up and empty, holding back
At loss you're forgotten
Getting back, get back
Get back, get back, yeah

Now realize, little sister
Overlooked little girl
No direction, little sister
Overlooked little girl
Change, change, change

WHAT'S THIS LIFE FOR?

Hurray for a child
That makes it through
If there's any way
Because the answer lies in you

They're laid to rest
Before they've known just what to do
Their souls are lost
Because they could never find

What's this life for? *[4X]*

I see your soul, it's kind of gray
You see my heart, you look away
You see my wrist, I know your pain
I know your purpose on your plane

Don't say a last prayer
Because you could never find

[Chorus]

But they ain't here anymore
Don't have to settle the score
'Cause we all live under the reign
Of one king

But they ain't here anymore
Don't have to settle no god----- score
'Cause we all live under the reign
I said, you know, of

One king
One king
One king

But they ain't here anymore
Don't have to settle no god----- score
'Cause we all live under the reign
I said, you know, of

One king
One king
One king

But they ain't here anymore
Don't have to settle no god----- score
'Cause we all live under the reign
Of one king

ONE

Affirmative may be justified
Take from one, give to another
The goal is to be unified
Take my hand, be my brother
The payments silenced the masses
Sanctified by oppression
Unity took a backseat
Sliding further into regression

One, oh one
The only way is one

One, oh one
The only way is one

I feel angry, I feel helpless
Want to change the world, yeah
I feel violent, I feel alone
Don't try and change my mind, no

Society blind by color
Why hold down one to raise another?
Discrimination now on both sides
Seeds of hate blossom further
The world is heading for mutiny
When all we want is unity
We may rise and fall, but in the end
We meet our fate together

One, oh one
The only way is one

One, oh one
The only way is one

I feel angry, I feel helpless
Want to change the world, yeah
I feel violent, I feel alone
Don't try and change my mind, no
[Repeat 2X]

I feel angry, I feel helpless
Want to change the world, yeah
I feel violent, I feel alone
Don't try and change my mind

HUMAN CLAY
Creed Album #2, 1999

ARE YOU READY?

Hey, Mr. Seeker, hold on to this advice
If you keep seeking you will find
Don't want to follow
Down roads been walked before
It's so hard to find unopened doors

Are you ready? Are you ready
For what's to come?
Oh I said, are you ready?
Are you ready
For what's to come?

Hey, Mr. Hero, walking a thin, fine line
Under the microscope of life
Remember your roots, my friend
They're right down below
'Cause heroes come and heroes go

Are you ready? Are you ready
For what's to come?
Oh I said, are you ready?
Are you ready
For what's to come?

Ten, nine, eight, seven, six, five, four, three, two, one
Count down to the change in life that's soon to come
Ten, nine, eight, seven, six, five, four, three, two, one
Count down to the change in life that's soon to come
Your life has just begun
Life has just begun
Life has just begun
Life has just begun

Are you ready? Are you ready
For what's to come?
Oh I said, are you ready?
Are you ready
For what's to come?
Oh I said, are you ready?
Are you ready
For what's to come?
Your life has just begun
Life has just begun
Life has just begun

WHAT IF

I can't find the rhyme in all my reason
Lost sense of time and all seasons
Feel I've been beaten down
By the words of men who have no grounds
Can't sleep beneath the trees of wisdom
When your ax has cut the roots that feed them
Forked tongues in bitter mouths
Can drive a man to bleed from inside out

What if you did?
What if you lied?
What if I avenge?
What if eye for an eye?

I've seen the wicked fruit of your vine
Destroy the man who lacks a strong mind
Human pride sings a vengeful song
Inspired by the times you've been walked on
My stage is shared by many millions
Who lift their hands up high because they feel this
We are one, we are strong
The more you hold us down the more we press on

What if you did?
What if you lied?
What if I avenge?
What if eye for an eye?

I know I can't hold the hate inside my mind
'Cause what consumes your thoughts controls your life
So I'll just ask a question
A lonely simple question
I'll just ask one question
What if? What if?
What if? What if?
What if I?

What if? What if?
What if? What if?
What if I?

What if? What if?
What if? What if?
What if I?

What if? What if?
What if? What if?
What if I?

What if you did?

What if you lied?
What if I avenge?
What if eye for an eye?

What if your words could be judged like a crime?

What if? What if?
What if? What if?
What if I?

What if? What if?
What if? What if?
What if I?

What if? What if?
What if? What if?
What if I?

What if? What if?
What if? What if?
What if I?

BEAUTIFUL

She wears a coat of color
Loved by some, feared by others
She's immortalized in young men's eyes

Lust she breeds in the eyes of brothers
Violent sons make bitter mothers
So close your eyes, here's your surprise

The beautiful is empty
Beautiful is free
Beautiful loves no one
Beautiful stripped me
Stripped me
Stripped me
She stripped me

In your mind she's your companion
Vile instincts often candid
Your regret is all that's left

The beautiful is empty
Beautiful is free
Beautiful loves no one
Beautiful stripped me
Stripped me
Stripped me
She stripped me

She told me where I'm going
And it's far away from home
I think I'll go there on my own
I think I'll go there on my own
She told me where I'm going
And it's far away from home
I think I'll go there on my own
I think I'll go there on my own

The beautiful is empty
Beautiful is free
Beautiful loves no one
Beautiful stripped me
Stripped me
Stripped me
She stripped me
She stripped me
Stripped me

SAY I

The dust has finally settled on the field of human clay
Just enough light has shone through
To tell the night from the day
We are incomplete and hollow
For our maker has gone away

Who is to blame?
We'll surely melt in the rain
Say I, say I
Say I, say I
Say I, say I

The stillness is so lifeless with no spirit in your soul
Like children with no vision do exactly what they're told
Being led into the desert
For your strength will surely fade

Who is to blame?
We'll surely melt in the rain
Say I, say I
Say I, say I
Say I, say I

Say I, say I
Say I, say I

Frantic, faction, focus
The world breathes
And out forms this misconception we call man
But I don't know him
No, I don't know him
Because he lies
They lie

Say I, yeah
Say I, yeah
Say I, yeah
Say I, say I
Say I, say I

WRONG WAY

What makes you touch?
What makes you feel?
What makes you stop and smell the roses in an open field?
What makes you unclean?
Yeah, yeah
Yeah, yeah

Yeah, yeah, yeah
Yeah, yeah

What makes you laugh?
What makes you cry?
What makes our youth run
From the thought that we might die?
What makes you bleed?
Yeah, yeah
Yeah, yeah
Yeah, yeah, yeah

Somebody told me the wrong way
Yeah, yeah
Yeah, yeah
Yeah, yeah, yeah
Somebody told me the wrong way

What if I died?
What did I give?
I hope it was an answer so you might live
I hope I helped you live
I hope I helped you live
I hope I helped you live
I hope I helped you live
Live

Yeah, yeah
Yeah, yeah
Yeah, yeah, yeah
Somebody told me the wrong way

Yeah, yeah
Yeah, yeah
Yeah, yeah, yeah
Somebody told me the wrong way

Yeah, yeah
Yeah, yeah
Yeah, yeah, yeah

FACELESS MAN

I spent a day by the river
It was quiet and the wind stood still
I spent some time with nature
To remind me of all that's real
It's funny how silence speaks sometimes when you're alone
And remember that you feel
I said, it's funny how silence speaks sometimes when you're alone
And remember that you feel

Again I stand, Lord, I stand
Against the Faceless Man
Again I stand, Lord, I stand
Against the Faceless Man

Now I saw a face on the water
It looked humble but willing to fight
I saw the will of a warrior
His yoke is easy and His burden is light

He looked me right in the eyes
Direct and concise to remind me
To always do what's right
He looked me right in the eyes
Direct and concise to remind me
To always do what's right

Again I stand, Lord, I stand
Against the Faceless Man
Again I stand, Lord God, I stand,
Against the Faceless Man

'Cause if the face inside can't see the light
I know I'll have to walk alone
And if I walk alone to the other side
I know I might not make it home

[Chorus]

Next time I see this face
I'll say I choose to live for always
So won't you come inside and never go away
Next time I see this face
I'll say I choose to live for always
So won't you come inside and never go away

[Chorus]

Again I stand, Lord, I stand
Against the Faceless Man

NEVER DIE

Hands on a window pane
Watching some children laugh and play
They're running in circles
With candy canes and French braids
Inspired to question
What makes us grown-ups anyway?
Let's search for the moment
When youth betrayed itself to age

So let the children play
Inside your heart always
And death you will defy
'Cause your youth will never die
Never die

In searching for substance
We're clouded by struggle's haze
Remember the meaning
Of playing out in the rain
We swim in the fountain
Of youth's timeless maze
If you drink the water
Your youth will never fade

So let the children play
Inside your heart always
And death you will defy
'Cause your youth will never die
Never die
Never die
Never die

I won't let go of that youthful soul
Despite body and mind my youth will never die
I won't let go of that youthful soul
Despite body and mind my youth will never die

So let the children play
Inside your heart always
And death you will defy
'Cause your youth will never die

So let the children play
Inside your heart always
And death you will defy
'Cause your youth will never die
Never die

WITH ARMS WIDE OPEN

Well, I just heard the news today
Seems my life is gonna change
I close my eyes, begin to pray
Then tears of joy stream down my face

With arms wide open
Under the sunlight
Welcome to this place
I'll show you everything
With arms wide open

With arms wide open

Well, I don't know if I'm ready
To be the man I have to be
I'll take a breath, I'll take her by my side
We stand in awe, we've created life

With arms wide open
Under the sunlight
Welcome to this place
I'll show you everything
With arms wide open
Now everything has changed
I'll show you love
I'll show you everything
With arms wide open

With arms wide open
I'll show you everything, oh yeah
With arms wide open
Wide open

If I had just one wish
Only one demand
I hope he's not like me
I hope he understands
That he can take this life
And hold it by the hand
And he can greet the world
With arms wide open

[Chorus 2]

With arms wide open
I'll show you everything, oh yeah
With arms wide open
Wide open

HIGHER

When dreaming I'm guided to another world
Time and time again
At sunrise I fight to stay asleep
'Cause I don't want to leave the comfort of this place
'Cause there's a hunger, a longing to escape
From the life I live when I'm awake
So let's go there
Let's make our escape
Come on, let's go there
Let's ask can we stay?

Can you take me higher?
To a place where blind men see
Can you take me higher?
To a place with golden streets

Although I would like our world to change
It helps me to appreciate
Those nights and those dreams
But, my friend, I'd sacrifice all those nights
If I could make the Earth and my dreams the same
The only difference is
To let love replace all our hate
So let's go there
Let's make our escape
Come on, let's go there
Let's ask can we stay?

[Chorus]

So let's go there, let's go there,
Come on, let's go there
Let's ask can we stay?

Up high I feel like I'm alive for the very first time
Set up high I'm strong enough to take these dreams
And make them mine

Set up high I'm strong enough to take these dreams
And make them mine

[Chorus 2X]

WASH AWAY THOSE YEARS

She came calling
One early morning
She showed her crown of thorns
She whispered softly
To tell a story
About how she had been wronged
As she lay lifeless
He stole her innocence
And this is how she carried on
This is how she carried on

Well I guess she closed her eyes
And just imagined everything's alright
But she could not hide her tears
'Cause they were sent to wash away those years
They were sent to wash away those years

My anger's violent
But still I'm silent
When tragedy strikes at home
I know this decadence is shared by millions
Remember you're not alone
Remember you're not alone

Well if you just close your eyes
And just imagine everything's alright
But do not hide your tears
'Cause they were sent to wash away those years
Well if you just close your eyes
And just imagine everything's alright
But do not hide your tears
'Cause they were sent to wash away those years
They were sent to wash away those years
Maybe we can wash away those years

For we have crossed many oceans
And we labor in between
In life there are many quotients
And I hope I find the mean
The mean, the mean

[Chorus 2]

I hope that you can wash away those years

INSIDE US ALL

When I'm all alone
And no one else is there
Waiting by the phone
To remind me
I'm still here
When shadows paint the scenes
Where spotlights used to fall
And I'm left wondering
Is it really worth it all?

There's a peace inside us all
Let it be your friend
It will help you carry on in the end
There's a peace inside us all

Life can hold you down
When you're not looking up
Can't you hear the sounds?
Hearts beating out loud
Although the names change
Inside we're all the same
Why can't we tear down these walls?
To show the scars we're covering

There's a peace inside us all
Let it be your friend
It will help you carry on in the end
There's a peace inside us all

There's a peace
Oh there's a peace inside us all
Let it be
Oh I said, let it be, let it be your friend
There's a peace inside us all
Let it be your friend
It will help you carry on in the end
There's a peace inside us all
There's a peace inside us all, inside us all
Let it be, let it be, let it be,
Let it be, let it be, let it be,
Let it be, let it be your friend

WEATHERED

Creed Album #3, 2001

BULLETS

Walking around I hear the sounds of the earth seeking relief
I'm trying to find a reason to live
But the mindless clutter my path
Oh these thorns in my side
Oh these thorns in my side
I know I have something free
I have something so alive
I think they shoot 'cause they want it
I think they shoot 'cause they want it
I think they shoot 'cause they want it

I feel forces all around me
Come on raise your head
Those who hide behind the shadows
Live with all that's dead

Look at me
Look at me
At least look at me when you shoot a bullet through my head
Through my head
Through my head
Through my head

In my lifetime when I'm disgraced
By jealousy and lies
I laugh aloud 'cause my life
Has gotten inside someone else's mind

[Chorus]

Hey all I want is what's real
Something I touch and can feel
I'll hold it close and never let it go
Said why, why do we live this life
With all this hate inside?
I'll give it away 'cause I don't want it no more
Please help me find a place
Somewhere far away
Yes, I'll go and you'll never see me again

[Chorus 2X]

Look at me
Look at me

FREEDOM FIGHTER

The mouths of envious
Always find another door
While at the gates of paradise they
Beat us down some more
But our mission's set in stone
'Cause the writing's on the wall
I'll scream it from the mountain tops
Pride comes before a fall

So many thoughts to share
All this energy to give
Unlike those who hide the truth
I tell it like it is
If the truth will set you free
I feel sorry for your soul
Can't you hear the ringing 'cause
For you the bell tolls

I'm just a freedom fighter
No remorse
Raging on in holy war
Soon there'll come a day
When you're face-to-face with me
Face-to-face with me

Can't you hear us coming?
People marching all around
Can't you see we're coming?
Close your eyes, it's over now
Can't you hear us coming?
The fight has only just begun
Can't you see we're coming?

I'm just a freedom fighter
No remorse
Raging on in holy war
Soon there'll come a day
When you're face-to-face with me
Face-to-face with me

WHO'S GOT MY BACK?

Run, hide
All that was sacred to us
Sacred to us
See the signs
The covenant has been broken
By mankind
Leaving us with no shoulder
With no shoulder
To rest our head on
To rest our head on
To rest our head on

Who's got my back now?
When all we have left is deceptive
So disconnected
So what is the truth now?

There's still time
All that has been devastated
Can be recreated
Realize
We pick up the broken pieces
Of our lives
Giving ourselves to each other
Ourselves to each other
To rest our head on
To rest our head on
To rest our head on

Who's got my back now?
When all we have left is deceptive
So disconnected
So what is the truth now?

Tell me the truth now
Tell us the truth now

Who's got my back now?
When all we have left is deceptive
So disconnected
So what is the truth now?

SIGNS

This is not about age
Time served on the earth doesn't mean you grow in mind
Grow in mind
This is not about God
Spiritual insinuations seem to shock our nation
Our nation, yeah

Come with me, I'm fading underneath the lights
Come with me, come with me, come with me now

This is not about race
It's a decision to stop the division in your life
In our lives
This is not about sex
We all know sex sells and the whole world is buying
You're buying, yeah

Come with me, I'm fading underneath the lights
Come with me, come with me, come with me now

Can't you see the signs?
See the signs now

Can't you see the signs?
See the signs now

Can't you see the signs?
See the signs now

Can't you see the signs?
See the signs now

Can't you see the signs?
See the signs now

Can't you see the signs?
See the signs now

Yeah, come on
Feel it
Yeah

Come with me, I'm fading underneath the lights
Come with me, come with me, come with me now

Can't you see them, see the signs, you see them, all the signs, we
    see them

Can't you see them, see the signs, you see them, all the signs, we
    see them

ONE LAST BREATH

Please come now, I think I'm falling
I'm holding on to all I think is safe
It seems I found the road to nowhere
And I'm trying to escape
I yelled back when I heard thunder
But I'm down to one last breath
And with it let me say
Let me say

Hold me now
I'm six feet from the edge and I'm thinking
That maybe six feet
Ain't so far down

I'm looking down now that it's over
Reflecting on all of my mistakes
I thought I found the road to somewhere
Somewhere in His grace
I cried out, heaven save me
But I'm down to one last breath
And with it let me say
Let me say

[Chorus 2X]

I'm so far down

Sad eyes follow me
But I still believe there's something left for me
So please come stay with me
'Cause I still believe there's something left for you and me
For you and me
For you and me

Hold me now
I'm six feet from the edge and I'm thinking

[Chorus]

Please come now, I think I'm falling
I'm holding on to all I think is safe

MY·SACRIFICE

Hello, my friend
We meet again
It's been a while
Where should we begin?
Feels like forever
Within my heart are memories
Of perfect love that you gave to me
Oh, I remember

When you are with me, I'm free
I'm careless, I believe
Above all the others we'll fly
This brings tears to my eyes
My sacrifice

We've seen our share
Of ups and downs
Oh, how quickly life
Can turn around
In an instant
It feels so good to reunite
Within yourself and within your mind
Let's find peace there

'Cause when you are with me, I'm free
I'm careless, I believe
Above all the others we'll fly
This brings tears to my eyes
My sacrifice

I just want to say hello again
I just want to say hello again

When you are with me, I'm free
I'm careless, I believe
Above all the others we'll fly
This brings tears to my eyes

'Cause when you are with me, I am free
I'm careless, I believe
Above all the others we'll fly
This brings tears to my eyes
My sacrifice, my sacrifice

I just want to say hello again
I just want to say hello again
My sacrifice

STAND HERE WITH ME

You always reached out to me and helped me believe
All those memories we share
I will cherish every one of them
The truth of it is there's a right way to live
And you showed me
So now you live on in the words of a song
You're a melody

You stand here with me now

Just when fear blinded me, you taught me to dream
I'll give you everything I am and still fall short of
What you've done for me
In this life that I live
I hope I can give love unselfishly
I've learned the world is bigger than me
You're my daily dose of reality

You stand here with me now

On and on we sing
On and on we sing this song

'Cause you stand here with me

WEATHERED

I lie awake on a long, dark night
I can't seem to tame my mind
Slings and arrows are killing me inside
Maybe I can't accept the life that's mine, no
Maybe I can't accept the life that's mine

Simple living is my desperate cry
Been trading love with indifference
And yeah, it suits me just fine
I try to hold on but I'm calloused to the bone
Maybe that's why I feel alone, yeah
Maybe that's why I feel so alone

'Cause me, I'm rusted and weathered
Barely holdin' together
I'm covered with skin that peels
And it just won't heal
I'm rusted and weathered
Barely holdin' together
I'm covered with skin that peels
And it just won't heal
No, it just won't heal

The sun shines and I can't avoid the light
I think I'm holding on to life too tight
Ashes to ashes and dust to dust
Sometimes I feel like giving up, yeah
I said, sometimes I feel like giving up

'Cause me, I'm rusted and weathered
Barely holdin' together
I'm covered with skin that peels
And it just won't heal
I'm rusted and weathered
Barely holdin' together
I'm covered with skin that peels
And it just won't heal
It just won't heal, no

The day reminds me of you
The night hides your truth
The earth is a voice
Speaking to you
Take all this pride
And leave it behind
Because one day it ends
One day we die
Believe what you will

That is your right
But I choose to win
I choose to fight
To fight

'Cause me, I'm rusted and weathered
Barely holdin' together
I'm covered with skin that peels
And it just won't heal
I'm rusted and weathered
Barely holdin' together
I'm covered with skin that peels
And it just won't
Covered with skin that peels
And it just won't
Covered with skin that peels
And it just won't heal

HIDE

To what do I owe this gift, my friend?
My life, my love, my soul?
I've been dancing with the devil way too long
And it's making me grow old
Making me grow old

Let's leave, oh let's get away
Get lost in time
Where there's no reason left to hide
Let's leave, oh let's get away
Run in fields of time
Where there's no reason left to hide
No reason to hide

What are you gonna do with your gift, dear child?
Give life, give love, give soul?
Divided is the one who dances
For the soul is so exposed
So exposed

Let's leave, oh let's get away
Get lost in time
Where there's no reason left to hide
Let's leave, oh let's get away
Run in fields of time
Where there's no reason left to hide
No reason to hide

There is no reason to hide
There is no reason to hide
There is no reason to hide
There is no reason to hide

Let's leave, oh let's get away
Get lost in time
Where there's no reason left to hide
Let's leave, oh let's get away
Run in fields of time
Where there's no reason left to hide, yeah

Let's leave, oh let's get away
Get lost in time
Where there's no reason left to hide

No reason to hide

There is no reason to hide
There is no reason to hide

DON'T STOP DANCING

At times life is wicked and I just can't see the light
A silver lining sometimes isn't enough
To make some wrongs seem right
Whatever life brings
I've been through everything
And now I'm on my knees again

But I know I must go on
Although I hurt I must be strong
Because inside I know that many feel this way

Children, don't stop dancing
Believe you can fly
Away, away

At times life's unfair and you know it's plain to see
Hey, God, I know I'm just a dot in this world
Have You forgot about me?
Whatever life brings
I've been through everything
And now I'm on my knees again

But I know I must go on
Although I hurt I must be strong
Because inside I know that many feel this way

[Chorus]

Am I hiding in the shadows?
Forget the pain and forget the sorrows

Am I hiding in the shadows?
Forget the pain and forget the sorrows

But I know I must go on
Although I hurt I must be strong
Because inside I know that many feel this way

[Chorus 3X]

Am I hiding in the shadows?
Are we hiding in the shadows?

LULLABY

Hush, my love, now don't you cry
Everything will be all right
Close your eyes and drift in dream
Rest in peaceful sleep

If there's one thing I hope I showed you
If there's one thing I hope I showed you
Hope I showed you

Just give love to all
Just give love to all
Just give love to all

Oh, my love, in my arms tight
Every day you give me life
As I drift off to your world
Rest in peaceful sleep

I know there's one thing that you showed me
I know there's one thing that you showed me
That you showed me

Just give love to all
Just give love to all
Just give love to all

Let's give love to all
Let's give love to all

Just give love to all
Let's give love to all
Just give love to all
Let's give love to all

FULL CIRCLE
Creed Album #4, 2009

OVERCOME

Don't cry victim to me
Everything we are and used to be
Is buried and gone
Now it's my turn to speak
It's my turn to expose and
Release what's been killing me
I'll be d----- fighting you
It's impossible, impossible
Say goodbye, with no sympathy

I'm entitled to overcome
Completely stunned and numb
Knock me down, throw me to the floor
There's no pain I can feel no more
I'm entitled to overcome
Overcome

Finally see what's beneath
Everything I am and hope to be
Cannot be lost
I'll be d----- fighting you
You're impossible, impossible
Say goodbye, with no sympathy

I'm entitled to overcome
Completely stunned and numb
Knock me down, throw me to the floor
There's no pain I can feel no more
I'm entitled to overcome
Overcome

Overcome

You'll never know what I was thinking before you came around
Take a step, take a breath, put your guard down
I cannot worry anymore of what you think of me
I may be crazy but I'm buried in your memory

I'm entitled to overcome
Completely stunned and numb
Knock me down, throw me to the floor
There's no pain I can feel no more
I'm entitled to overcome
Completely stunned and numb
I'm entitled to overcome
Completely stunned and numb
I'm entitled to overcome

I may be crazy but I'm buried in your memory

BREAD OF SHAME

If you say I'm alive I guess I'm living
Why should I guess your size, a choice I've been given
Tell me everything's fine and peace is coming
I won't listen to the heartache I'm numbing

When the world casts me down and says I've changed
I'll survive on all the promises you made to me
Guess there's no one to blame
When all you're living on is bread of shame
Bread of shame
When the world says I've changed
Bread of shame
Just promise me fame, I'll survive on the bread of shame

As long as you say I'm free
Then keep these chains on me
Tell me down is up
I'll let you fill this broken cup
When the world fall down
Let them fall on me
'Cause no one's around who believe me

When the world casts me down and says I've changed
I'll survive on all the promises you made to me
Guess there's no one to blame
When all you're living on is bread of shame
Bread of shame
When the world says I've changed
Bread of shame
Just promise me fame, I'll survive on the bread of shame

Tell me where I sign my name
Inside I find no peace of mind to hide behind
Only bread of shame
Tell me where I sign my name
Inside I have no peace of mind
Only bread of shame

Bread of shame
When the world says I've changed
Bread of shame
Just promise me fame, I'll survive on the bread of shame

A THOUSAND FACES

I stand surrounded by the walls that once confined me
Knowing I'll be underneath them
When they crumble, when they fall
With clarity my scars remind me
Ash still simmers just under my skin

Indifference smiles again
So much I hide
How is stepping back a move forward?

Now I'm forced to look behind
I'm forced to look at you
You wear a thousand faces
Tell me, tell me which is you
Broken mirrors paint the floor
Why can't you see the truth?
You wear a thousand faces
Tell me, tell me which is you
Tell me which is you

Eerily time made no change
Pointing fingers, laying blame
Lying over and over and over and over
Deceiving your mind
Dug my grave, trashed my name
Yet here I stand, so you won't fade away
Indifference smiles again
So much I hide
How is stepping back a move forward?

Now I'm forced to look behind
I'm forced to look at you
You wear a thousand faces
Tell me, tell me which is you
Broken mirrors paint the floor
Why can't you see the truth?
You wear a thousand faces
Tell me, tell me which is you
Tell me which is you

I bleed inside
Just let it out
Just let it out
I bleed inside
Just let it out
Just let it out

Now I'm forced to look behind
I'm forced to look at you
You wear a thousand faces
Tell me, tell me which is you
Broken mirrors paint the floor
Why can't you tell the truth?
You wear a thousand faces
Tell me, tell me which is you

Tell me
Tell me
Tell me

You wear a thousand faces
Tell me which is you
Tell me which is you

SUDDENLY

A nature to nurture
An instinct to sin
What's underneath the skin you live in?
You trade your unlimited
Your precious creation
You will submit
You will get it

Suddenly I have no strength at all
So suddenly hit with all I've lost
Suddenly my world is falling apart
So suddenly, so suddenly
Suddenly

You say you're a victim
But that's just a symptom
You're so very clear
You volunteered
Why are you fighting, just stop your denying
Own up to the sin
You bury within

Suddenly I have no strength at all
So suddenly hit with all I've lost
Suddenly my world is falling apart
So suddenly, so suddenly
Suddenly

I have no strength at all
I've been hit with a loss
So suddenly my world falls apart
I have no strength at all
I've been hit with a loss
Suddenly my world falls apart
My world falls apart

Suddenly I have no strength at all
So suddenly hit with all I've lost
Suddenly my world is falling apart
So suddenly, so suddenly

Suddenly I have no strength at all
So suddenly hit, so suddenly hit
Suddenly my world falls apart
So suddenly, so suddenly
Suddenly

Suddenly my world falls apart
My world falls apart
My world

RAIN

Can you help me out, can you lend me a hand?
It's safe to say that I'm stuck again
Trapped between this life and the light
I just can't figure out how to make it right

A thousand times before
I've wondered if there's something more
Something more

I feel it's gonna rain like this for days
So let it rain down and wash everything away
I hope that tomorrow the sun will shine
With every tomorrow comes another life

I feel it's gonna rain, for days and days
I feel it's gonna rain

I tried to figure out, I can't understand
What it means to be whole again
Trapped between the truth and the consequence
Nothing's real, nothing's making sense

A thousand times before
I've wondered if there's something more
Something more

I feel it's gonna rain like this for days
So let it rain down and wash everything away
I hope that tomorrow the sun will shine
I feel it's going to rain like this, rain like this, rain like this

Fall down, wash away my yesterdays
Fall down, so let the rain fall down on me

I feel it's gonna rain like this for days
Let it rain down and wash everything away
I hope that tomorrow the sun will shine
I feel it's going to rain like this, rain like this

So let the rain fall
I feel it's gonna rain like this, rain like this
So let the rain fall down
I feel it's gonna rain like this
I feel it's gonna rain

AWAY IN SILENCE

You walked away in silence
You walked away to breathe
Stopped and turned around to say goodbye to me
I'm pleading as you're leaving, I'm begging you stay
I'm not the man I used to be, I've changed
I'm not the man I used to be, I've changed

Don't give up on us, don't give up on love *[2X]*
If my life is the price, then my life it will cost
Now that I'm picking up the pieces see the pain that I have caused
It's hard to believe in someone you thought was lost
Don't give up on us, don't give up on love
Don't you walk away in silence

In tears you counted reasons
Tears covered you it seemed
Face down screaming, "God, help me please"
I'm pleading as you're leaving, I'm begging you to stay
I'm not the man I used to be, I've changed
I'm not the man I used to be, I've changed

Don't give up on us, don't give up on love *[2X]*
If my life is the price, then my life it will cost
It will cost my life

Now that I'm picking up the pieces see the pain that I have caused
It's hard to believe in someone you thought was lost
Don't give up on us, don't give up on love
Don't you walk away in silence
Please come back to me
Don't you walk away in silence
I'm not the man I used to be

Well I pray that tomorrow you'll be home
We can rebuild and forever we can go on
Go on, and go on
We can go on, well I pray that tomorrow you'll be home
Look at horizons and let the light bring you home, bring you home

Don't give up on us, don't give up on love *[2X]*
If my life is the price, then my life it will cost
Now that I'm picking up the pieces see the pain that I have caused
It's hard to believe in someone you thought was lost
Don't give up on us, don't give up on love
Don't walk away in silence
Please don't walk away
Don't you walk away in silence
I'm not the man I used to be

FEAR

The cradle of civilization sparks my fascination
Truth ignites our generation to change what's been programmed
Inside the mind
Don't you turn a blind eye
Change what's been programmed inside
Don't you turn a blind eye

Listen to me when I tell you
Feel the passion in my breath
Stay on top if they let you
'Cause the change is permanent
Change is permanent

Rudiments of interpersonal communication
Truth will uproot and bring war's devastation to light
Don't you turn a blind eye
Change what's been programmed inside
Staying silent is a crime

[Chorus]

Change starts in your mind
Leave the past behind
Forget everything you know
Make a change, let go

Change starts in your mind
Leave the past behind
Forget everything you know
Make a change, let go

Change starts in your mind
Leave the past behind
Forget everything you know
Make a change, let go
Let go, let go, let go, let go

[Chorus 2X]

Leave the past behind
Leave the past behind
Make a change, let go
Let go, let go, let go, let go, let go

ON MY SLEEVE

The eyes around me are so cold
With every chance they steal my soul
So walk with me, talk with me
Hold my hand, I'm stumbling
In consequence here is me alive

Can you fix what's made to be broken?
I can't fix what's made to be

My heart is tattooed on my sleeve
I'm not hiding, no
It only hurts to breathe
My heart is tattooed on my sleeve
I know it's blinding, oh
It only hurts to breathe

Standing now, I'm alone
I need answers, tell me everything you know
So heavy is the night, exhausted
Whispers tend to crucify my mind
I'm fighting but I'm blind

Can you fix what's made to be broken?
I can't fix what's made to be

My heart is tattooed on my sleeve
I'm not hiding, no
It only hurts to breathe
My heart is tattooed on my sleeve
I know it's blinding, oh
It only hurts
It only hurts
It only hurts to breathe

I shout out
Can you hear me?
Mistakes have cost me years
Do they cost you?
Are you like me?
Tell me, please

My heart is tattooed on my sleeve
I'm not hiding, no
It only hurts to breathe
My heart is tattooed on my sleeve
I know it's blinding, oh
It only hurts
It only hurts
It only hurts to breathe

FULL CIRCLE

Got your freedom now, boy
Who do you serve?
Took for granted what you should have preserved
No time left, no time left to make amends
Keep burning bridges while you're buying your new friends
A day of reflection hits, you're a shell, skin and bones, counting
    costs
Is it worth your soul?
A day of reflection hits

It's funny how times can change, rearrange, and distance makes
The pain fade away
So important then, doesn't matter now
Both feet on the ground
Come full circle, yeah, come full circle

No access granted now, boy, you've been denied
Jump a fence to see what's on the other side
Are you wanted, are you wanted
The question is, could second chances mean another impression?
A day of reflection hits, you're a shell, skin and bones, counting
    costs
Is it worth your soul?
A day of reflection hits

It's funny how times can change, rearrange, and distance makes
The pain fade away
So important then, doesn't matter now
Both feet on the ground
Come full circle, we've come full circle

I got one foot stuck in heaven, yeah
One boot stuck in hell
I looked at God, He winked at me
I made this mess myself
Don't be surprised and don't deny
Hear every word I say
Close the door and don't look back or you will fade away

It's funny how times can change, rearrange, and distance makes
The pain fade away

It's funny how times can change, rearrange, and distance makes
The pain fade away
So important then, doesn't matter now
Both feet on the ground
Come full circle, full circle, come full circle
We have come full circle

TIME

I can't explain
Can't quite put my finger on it
The difference that makes us so different
We've said everything
Our words only betrayed us
Nothing is left, nothing was left unsaid

This time I have nothing left to lose
I'm stuck, the second hand won't move
It's about time that I speak my mind
It's about time, about time I find
Pieces of me I have lost
Without any choice I move on
Hey, time, you're no friend of mine
Hey, time, you're no friend of mine

You cover yourself, you cover your skin
Your cover yourself like you cover your sin
Please untie my hands
I'm a sinner, I'm a man
I ask for one minute to make you understand

This time I have nothing left to lose
I'm stuck, the second hand won't move
It's about time that I speak my mind
It's about time, about time I find
Pieces of me I have lost
Without any choice I move on
Hey, time, you're no friend of mine
Hey, time, you're no friend of mine

Will you be there
To catch me when I stumble, when I fall?
When I fall
It's so very clear
You left me when I had no one at all
No one at all

Who will be there
To catch me, to catch me when I stumble
When I fall, when I fall?
It's so very clear
You left me, you left me with no one at all
No one at all
This time I have nothing left to lose
I'm stuck, the second hand won't move
It's about time that I speak my mind
It's about time, about time I find
Pieces of me I have lost

Without any choice I move on
Hey, time, you're no friend of mine
Hey, time, you're no friend of mine

No friend of mine
Time, you're no friend of mine
You're no friend of mine
Hey, time, you're no friend of mine
Hey, time, you're no friend of mine

The pieces of me I have lost
Without any choice I move on
Time
Time, you're no friend of mine

GOOD FIGHT

I give my all, my everything
Anything you want I strive to be
I tried, God knows I tried
Or am I stuck somewhere between
Who I am and who I hope to be?
Am I fighting the good fight?

Keep pressing on
Fight the good fight
Fight what you know is wrong
Keep pressing on
Fight the good fight
Fight what you know is wrong

I've come so far to fall too fast
Eyes forward, I can't look back, I try
God knows I try
I shift my eyes to the sky
In the distance see the horizon line
She waits for me
Fighting the good fight

[Chorus]

I give my all, my everything
Anything you want I strive to be
Am I stuck somewhere between
Who I am and who I hope to be?
Fighting, I'm fighting
Fighting the good fight
Am I stuck somewhere in between
Who I am and who I hope to be?

[Chorus]

Remember that
Sometimes I fall in between
The night's blue moon and the shadows it keeps
Fight on, fight the good fight
What you know is wrong
And I'll keep fighting
Fight on, keep fighting the good fight
Fight on, fight on
Fight on, keep fighting the good fight
Fight on, fight on

THE SONG YOU SING

Woke up and had a face to face
Guess my reflection had a lot to say
Why let my worries steal my days
It just brings me down

Does the song you sing
Have enough meaning?
Inspire us to sing along
Does the song you sing
Keep echoing?
Inspire us to sing the song you sing

What's wrong with the world today?
Tell me, what's all the talk about?
Lately I've been in a real bad place
Can't let the world bring me down

Does the song you sing
Have enough meaning?
Inspire us to sing along
Does the song you sing
Keep echoing?
Inspire us to sing the song you sing

I hope
The words I wrote
Keep calling out
Keep calling out
Forever let them sing
That song you sing, that song you sing

I hope
The words I wrote
Keep calling out
Keep calling out
Forever let them ring
Hear them echoing, hear them echoing

Does the song you sing
Have enough meaning?
Inspire us to sing along
Does the song you sing
Keep echoing?
Inspire us to sing the song you sing

The song you sing, the song you sing
It's the song you sing, it's the life you bring

That's why I sing the song you sing

Acknowledgments

SCOTT STAPP WOULD LIKE TO THANK:

David Ritz, Hayat "Yuma" Nesheiwat, Julia Nesheiwat, Dr. Janette Nesheiwat, Dina Nesheiwat, Daniel Nesheiwat, JonPaul Nesheiwat, Uncle Sam Zeidan, Matt Fuller, Miriam Chow, Steve Dias, Pastor Rick Berlin, Jimmy Weiss, Jimmy Mooney, Dr. Robert Mooney, Raymond Scott, John Flood, Jeff Stilwell, Michael Guido, Renee Karalian, Joe Tacopina, David Bercuson, Steve Leber, Jordan Leber, Ken Fermaglich, Diana Meltzer, Irving Azoff, Brent Look, Tresa Patterson, Michelle Soudry, Creed, and all my amazing fans.

DAVID RITZ WOULD LIKE TO THANK:

Scott Stapp, courageous artist, brother in Christ; David Vigliano; Ron Beers; Carol Traver; Lisa Jackson; Stephanie Rische; Dejon Mayes; David Koff; Dennis Franklin; Dave Stein; Herb Powell; Ian Valentine; John Tayloe; Juan Moscoso; Kevin King; Skip Smith; Richard Cohen; Richard Freed; Harry Weinger; my loving wife and lifelong girlfriend, Roberta; my daughters, Alison and Jessica; my brother-sons, Jim and Henry; my grandkids, Charlotte, Nins, James, and Isaac; my sisters, Esther and Elizabeth; my wonderful dad; and my beautiful nieces and nephews. Thank you, Jesus.

About the Authors

SCOTT STAPP is among the most successful artists of the modern rock era. As Creed's lead vocalist, he has sold more than forty million records and has performed in sold-out arenas the world over. One *Rolling Stone* writer called Stapp "one of the most influential and boldest rock writer/performers of the past twenty-five years whose fans must be counted in the legions."

Stapp recorded four albums with Creed—*My Own Prison* (1997), *Human Clay* (1999), *Weathered* (2001), and *Full Circle* (2009)—each of which has been certified multiplatinum. In 2000 Stapp's song "With Arms Wide Open" won the Grammy for Best Rock Song of the Year, and in 2005 his first solo album, *The Great Divide*, was certified double platinum.

He is also the founder of the With Arms Wide Open Foundation, a charitable organization dedicated to "promoting healthy, loving relationships between children and their families."

Scott lives in Florida with his wife, Jaclyn (Miss New York USA of 2004, Mrs. Florida America of 2008, and award-winning author), and their three young children, Jagger, Milan, and Daniel.

DAVID RITZ has written books with Ray Charles, Marvin Gaye, Aretha Franklin, B. B. King, and many others. David is a born-again

Christian, and his book on black Christianity, *Messengers*, was called "inspirational and deeply moving" by *Time* magazine. He has won a Grammy for liner notes and is the only four-time winner of the Gleason Music Book of the Year Award. Ritz lives in Los Angeles with Roberta, his wife of forty-two years.

FREE
SONG DOWNLOAD

Download your exclusive copy of Scott's newest original song, "Sinner's Creed." Visit SINNERSCREED.COM and type in the code below:

This is a limited-time offer through DECEMBER 31, 2012

CP0602